The Ultimate SHERLOCK HOLMES PUZZLE BOOK

★ ★ ★

SOLVE OVER 140 PUZZLES FROM HIS MOST FAMOUS CASES

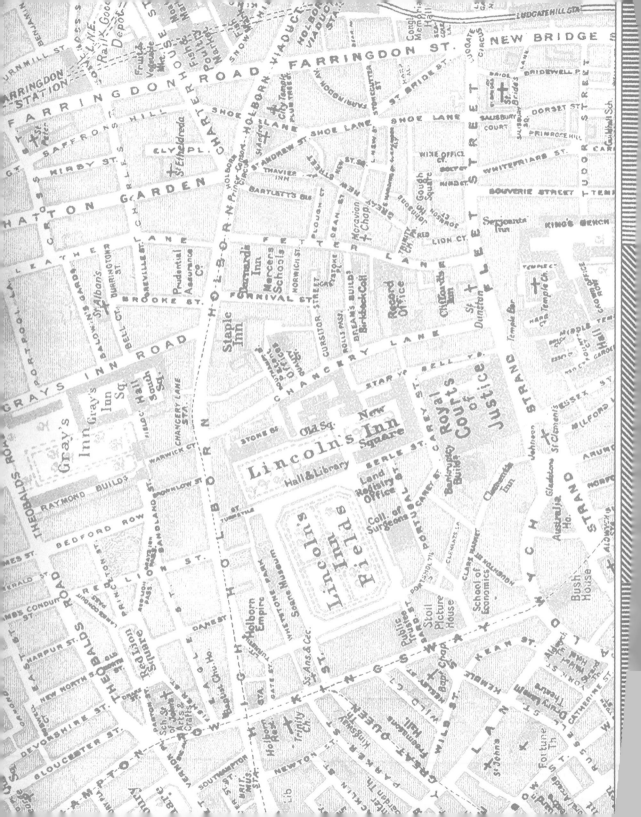

Brimming with creative inspiration, how-to projects, and useful information to enrich your everyday life, Quarto Knows is a favorite destination for those pursuing their interests and passions. Visit our site and dig deeper with our books into your area of interest: Quarto Creates, Quarto Cooks, Quarto Homes, Quarto Lives, Quarto Drives, Quarto Explores, Quarto Gifts, or Quarto Kids.

First published in 2021 by Wellfleet, an imprint of The Quarto Group, 142 West 36th Street, 4th Floor, New York, NY 10018, USA

T (212) 779-4972 F (212) 779-6058 www.QuartoKnows.com

Wellfleet titles are also available at discount for retail, wholesale, promotional and bulk purchase. For details, contact the Special Sales Manager by email at specialsales@quarto.com or by mail at The Quarto Group, Attn: Special Sales Manager, 100 Cummings Center Suite, 265D, Beverly, MA 01915, USA.

For their invaluable help, I also wish to thank Louise Wallace, Mike Dickman, and Stuart Miller.

10 9 8 7 6 5 4 3 2 1

ISBN: 978-1-57715-212-5

Publisher: Rage Kindelsperger
Creative Director: Laura Drew
Managing Editor: Cara Donaldson
Senior Editor: Erin Canning
Cover Design: Beth Middleworth
Interior Design: Didier Guiserix and Bernard Myers
Art: Bernard Myers and Didier Guiserix
London Map: Nicku/Shutterstock.com
Game Concept and Book Design: Pierre Berloquin – Créalude

Printed in China

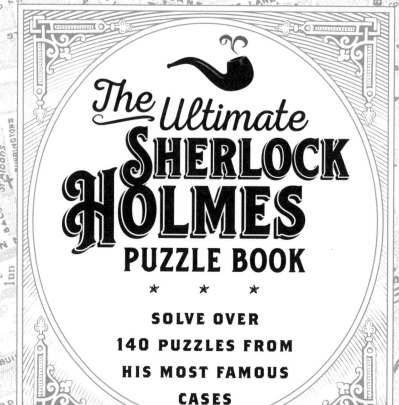

The *Ultimate* SHERLOCK HOLMES PUZZLE BOOK

★ ★ ★

SOLVE OVER 140 PUZZLES FROM HIS MOST FAMOUS CASES

PIERRE BERLOQUIN
PUZZLES BY BERNARD MYERS

WELLFLEET

Contents

Introduction

Puzzling One's Way About

Instead of reading each chapter chronologically, page after page—as you would in a traditional book—enjoy this adventure in the company of Sherlock Holmes and his loyal companion, Dr. Watson, jumping around each chapter while following the clues, just as our famous detective does when solving a case!

1 The Puzzle Challenge: Each chapter contains twenty-four puzzles for you to solve, in which Holmes and Watson react to famous characters, surroundings, and unusual events that were inspired by six classic Sherlock Holmes stories. For extra enjoyment, the plots have been slightly reimagined to add further mystery and purposely create more hurdles than Holmes and Watson had to overcome in the original stories. The puzzles will test your Sherlockian reasoning, with some being easier than others. And if you get stuck, you can always turn to the puzzle solutions in the back of the book.

2 The Map Challenge: Each chapter contains a map. After you solve a puzzle, consult the box at the bottom of the page, which will give you a clue for your next stop on the map. This destination will then tell you the number and name of the next puzzle you must solve. As mentioned earlier, you will jump around the chapter solving the puzzles, just as Holmes races from one point to another, following his flair for reasoning. If you get into any trouble, you can always check that you are on the right path by turning to the map solutions in the back of the book.

3 The Sherlock Challenge: This challenge encompasses the entire book. Next to certain map-clue boxes, you will come upon Sherlock's magnifying glass with a number in it. When you see this, turn to pages 176–177, where there is an empty grid for each chapter. There, follow the instructions, and when all the grids have been completed, you can discover a Sherlock Holmes quotation.

Best of luck with your adventure!

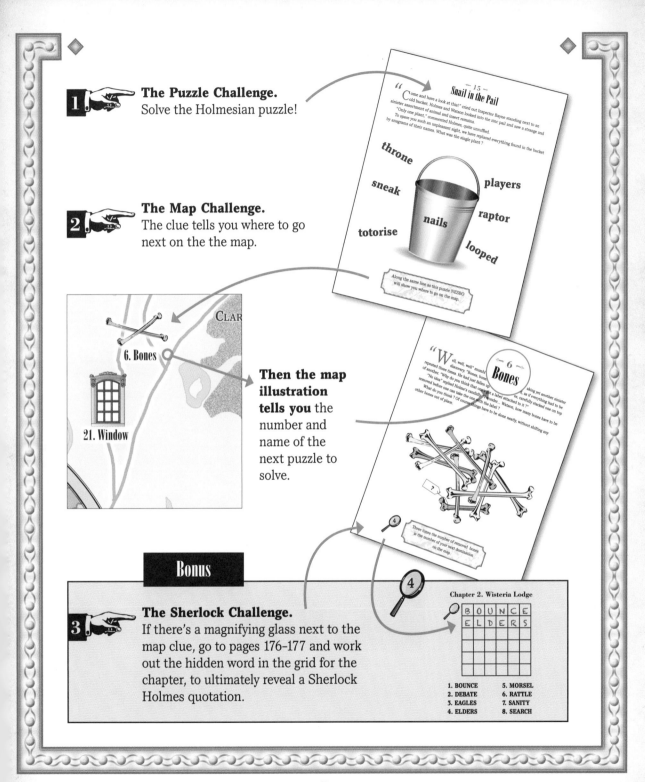

1 **The Puzzle Challenge.**
Solve the Holmesian puzzle!

2 **The Map Challenge.**
The clue tells you where to go next on the the map.

Then the map illustration tells you the number and name of the next puzzle to solve.

Bonus

3 **The Sherlock Challenge.**
If there's a magnifying glass next to the map clue, go to pages 176-177 and work out the hidden word in the grid for the chapter, to ultimately reveal a Sherlock Holmes quotation.

— 15 —
Snail in the Pail
"Come and have a look at this!" cried out Inspector Bayne standing next to an old bucket. Holmes and Watson looked into the zinc pail and saw a strange and sinister assortment of animal and insect remains.
"Only one plant," commented Holmes, quite unruffled.
"To spare you such an unpleasant sight, we have replaced everything found in the bucket by anagrams of their names. What was the single plant?"

throne
sneak
players
raptor
nails
totorise
looped

Along the same line as this puzzle NESBO will show you where to go on the map.

CLAR

6. Bones

21. Window

— 6 —
Bones
"Well, well, well" mumbled repeated three times. He had just fallen upon another... "Why do you think that..." "No idea," replied Holmes's candid... removed before one can take the one... aking yet another sinister as if everything had to be , carefully stacked one on top wonder... Watson, how many bones have to be other bones out of place. What do you think? Of course, things have to be done neatly, without shifting any

Three times the number of removed bones is the number of your next destination on the map.

Chapter 2. Wisteria Lodge

B	O	U	N	C	E
E	L	D	E	R	S

1. BOUNCE   5. MORSEL
2. DEBATE   6. RATTLE
3. EAGLES   7. SANITY
4. ELDERS   8. SEARCH

CHAPTER 1

The Mazarin Stone

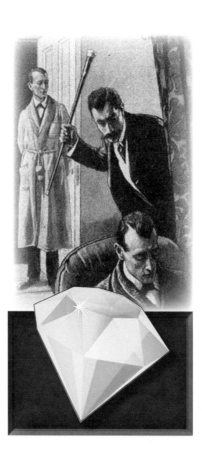

"The Adventure of the Mazarin Stone" has a striking difference from almost all the other Sherlock Holmes stories: it is not told by Watson. The adventure is written in the third person, and Watson is absent most of the time. The reason for this unique treatment is that Sir Arthur Conan Doyle initially wrote the story as a play. Another result of this story's origin is that the action takes place entirely in one setting, Sherlock's untidy Baker Street room. The story begins with a touch of nostalgia, with Watson looking around the room, memories springing back at him as he muses over familiar objects. However, action soon takes over, and while Sherlock Holmes solves his way through this case at the risk of his life, you will accompany him by solving related puzzles.

As explained in the introduction, use the map on pages 10–11 as a travel map. It will be essential to guide you through the strange places and events of this story to the final solving of the case.

Start with the first puzzle on page 12. Once you have solved it, follow the clue in the box at the bottom of the page to find your next destination on the map. This location comes with a number that gives you the number of the next puzzle you need to solve. Continue in this way, going back and forth, from puzzle to map, until you reach the last puzzle of the adventure. Have fun on your journey!

The Mazarin Stone

START

1. The Silhouette in the Window

6. Baker Street Blues

7. Who's Being Followed?

3. Parasol Pips

22. Music for a While

8. Card Bluff

17. Three Gentlemen

10. Clink

16. Action!

12. Terms of Address

20. Count Sylvius' Mustache

15. Clash of Opposites

5. The Precious Gem

24. A Grumpy Visitor

21. Being Murdered

N NE NW E W SE SW S

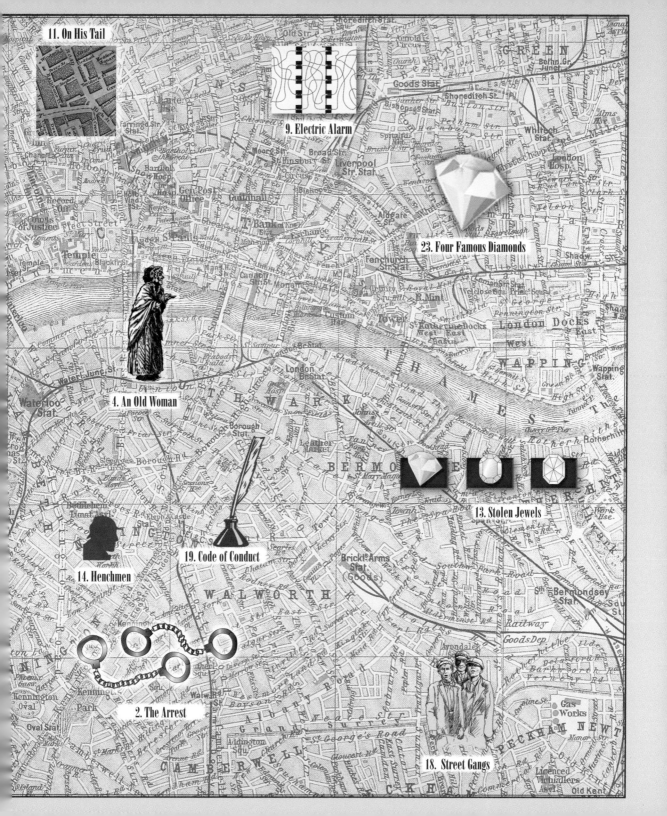

11. On His Tail

9. Electric Alarm

23. Four Famous Diamonds

4. An Old Woman

13. Stolen Jewels

19. Code of Conduct

14. Henchmen

2. The Arrest

18. Street Gangs

The Silhouette in the Window

To deceive his enemies, Holmes has a wax model of himself made to scale, which he places in front of the window. The decoy gives the impression that Holmes is quietly reading at home in his armchair, but in fact, he is in town investigating.

Every little detail counts, as with the silhouettes above. Only one is a perfect likeness of the original. Which one?

Watson has a touch of "Baker Street Blues" at the sight of a violin. Find this instrument on the map.

The Arrest

H olmes has accomplished his mission. Now it is time for the police to take over. Unfortunately, the handcuffs are tangled together. If you take the handcuff with the arrow, how many will come with it?

The next destination on the map leads
to a discontented fellow, but not because
he is wearing handcuffs.

Parasol Pips

To demonstrate that he was indeed the person who had followed him the previous day, Holmes shows Count Sylvius the parasol that was part of his disguise. The Count is furious, and has no time to admire the clever object. The black and white pips (dots) on this parasol are not randomly placed. They follow a Holmesian logic!

Can you figure out how many black and white pips there should be in the bare segment of this parasol?

Another object with pips
shows you where to go
on the map.

An Old Woman

HAMPER
TRENCH
BUTTER
MULLET
SWEARS
SCALPED
SALOON
CHAMP
SHADE
BRASH

Holmes wants to follow the suspects himself, but being so famous, he has to hide his identity. One of his disguises is dressing up as an old woman. Often, just a little detail can completely transform a person. And with words, it is just the same. A single letter changed and the word becomes unrecognizable.

All the words in the list above can be transformed into names of tools by changing just one letter. All, that is, except for one. Which one?

The stolen jewels on the map
will lead you to the £100,000
burglary mystery.

The Precious Gem

Sherlock Holmes doesn't function quite like anyone else. At the moment of his triumph, holding the stolen gem out in front of him, you would expect him to be filled with pride and satisfaction, but no, he begins thinking about the complex structure of cut diamonds.

   In the diamond shape below, the numbers follow a specific logic. Can you determine what numbers should replace the question marks?

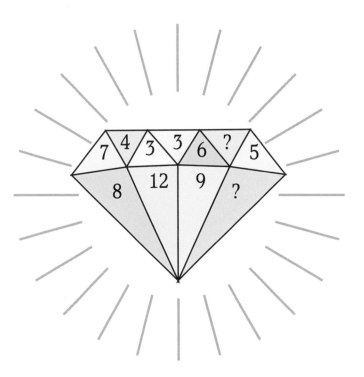

The number you found in the upper triangle, multiplied by two, is the next destination on the map.

Baker Street Blues

Watson hasn't been to Holmes' Baker Street room in a while, and the sight of the familiar objects makes him feel a touch nostalgic.

Can you decipher Watson's nostalgic feeling by placing the letters in the columns below the grid in the corresponding squares above? The difficulty is finding the right order. Black squares come between words.

W	A	T	S	O	N	■	L				■				■				■		
	■					C									■							
			■		■		I				■				■		V					
		-			■				-							L						

```
E  A  T  C  C  A  F  E  C  F  E  D  C  A  A  L  N  D  C  A  H  E  I  B
E  I  C  H  I  E  N  L  I  H  H  E  I  C  H  A  R  T  S  H  E  T  T  L  E
L  N  N  S  O  N  S  T  O  O  I  E     C  O  L  S     S     T  T  Y  T  H
W     S     O        T  K  M        R  O  U        T        U        O
```

 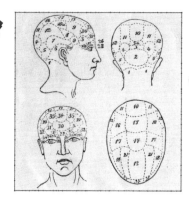 

There are four famous diamonds, but you only need to find one of them on the map.

Who's Being Followed?

Under various disguises, Sherlock Holmes has been spying on Count Sylvius and his accomplices as they go about their business.

Can you figure out who he has been following using the information below?

- If it's a man, he has a hat.
- If it's a woman, she is holding something.
- If it's someone with a hat, they also have a flower.
- If the person is holding something, they don't have a cane.
- If the person is wearing a necklace or a tie, you can see their shoes.

There are three of them, very proper and very important. That's the clue for where to go on the map.

Card Bluff

Holmes compares his conversation with Count Sylvius to a game of cards, in which each player tries to play his hand to outwit the other. By cleverly maneuvering his opponent, Holmes deduces the Count's cards.

In just the same way, you can find a similarity within the three hands below, even though one of the players has rather stupidly placed a card facedown. Can you determine the suit and value of this card?

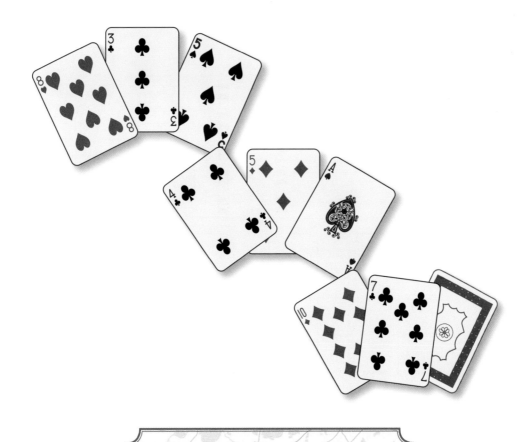

Multiply the value of the card by five and
go to that number on the map.

Electric Alarm

Watson cannot believe that a diamond as precious as the Mazarin Stone was not under sufficient protection.

"But it was!" explains Sherlock. "The place is equipped with the most modern of electric alarms. The only problem is that it had a major failure. In the circuit room, a master connector controls the whole system. Our thieves managed to remove it, and all protection ceased."

Which connector did they remove? Lodged in X, it should connect A to A, B to B, and so on.

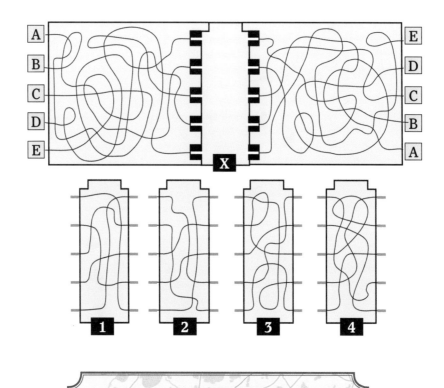

Multiply the number of the correct connector by six and then take away one for where to go on the map.

Clink

Holmes tries to convince Count Sylvius to give up the Mazarin Stone by explaining to him how many years he will spend in prison. To make his point, Holmes breaks down the Count's previous thefts below and how long each sentence will be.

"Although the tiara you stole from Princess Eliza was worth less than what you had hoped for, its worth of £1,000 will still give you 28 weeks and 4 days of prison time.

"Then, there was Lady Mathilda's necklace, which was estimated at £1,830, and will earn you a year and a day in prison.

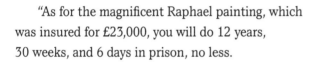

"As for the magnificent Raphael painting, which was insured for £23,000, you will do 12 years, 30 weeks, and 6 days in prison, no less.

"So, be reasonable and hand me the Mazarin Stone. Work out the prison time yourself, which corresponds to the £100,000 diamond!"

Without going into detail of weeks and days, can you figure out how many years in prison Count Sylvius will have to serve for the Mazarin Stone?

Take the correct answer in years, divide by three, and then add four years. That figure corresponds to your next stop on the map.

After leaving Sherlock Holmes, Watson suspected that someone was following him, so he took a roundabout route to his destination. He was right, a man was tailing him. Below is the last section of the report the person tailing him made. Where was Watson going?

"The doctor set out straight ahead and then turned left, and left again. He walked on up to Broad Street. There, he turned west and took the third street on the left. He looked around suspiciously but continued calmly down the street, and then, suddenly, he dashed up a narrow alleyway on the left. I thought I had lost him, but at the end of the alley, I saw his silhouette advancing southwards. At the T-junction, he turned left, crossed the following street, and took a road opposite, in a northeasterly direction. He probably thought he'd gotten rid of anyone tailing him, for he walked calmly straight on, taking another street almost straight ahead, slightly to his right, and continued on until he came to Broad Street again. He turned right and took the fourth left. At the end of that street, he reached his destination."

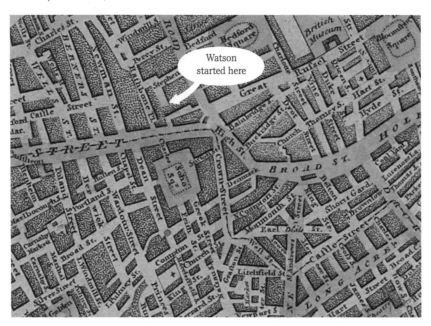

Watson started here

Find out who else is being followed on the travel
map and go there.

Terms of Address

When Count Sylvius becomes too familiar and addresses the famous detective simply as "Holmes," he is promptly reprimanded: "Count Sylvius, kindly give me my prefix when you address me."

Later, Watson teases his friend on his formalism and goes on to consider various forms of address. "How about the following list?" he asks.

"Dear Doctor, did you notice that in this list you can delete three of the titles and still have all the letters of the alphabet?" replies the detective.

Which three titles?

YOUR LORDSHIP

CITIZEN

THE VERY REVEREND

HIS EXCELLENCY

MY LADY BARONESS

THE CROWN PRINCE

HIS GRACIOUS HIGHNESS

THE RIGHT HONORABLE

THE DUKE OF . . .

HER MAJESTY THE QUEEN

A fashionable sunshade indicates the next stop on the map.

Stolen Jewels

The Mazarin Stone was, of course, the most precious trophy of Count Sylvius' heist. But while the thieves were at it, they also pocketed a few other jewels, and that's how the total adds up to exactly £100,000!

Which of the precious stones below did they also steal?

The Mazarin Stone
£90,000

Prince of Thornshire
£5,700

El Distio
£4,500

Bleintheim
£3,700

Duke Thriswick
£3,200

The Gartle Stone
£2,000

Poseidon
£1,800

Arbuth Prince
£1,500

Go to the electric alarm on the map.
Its complex circuitry should be
unmistakable.

Henchmen

Unscrupulous crooks, like Count Sylvius, always have their loyal henchmen. These are not particularly bright fellows, but their bosses can't do without them. Holmes has recently noticed that a number of high-flying crooks have joined forces, and they have come with their own dark accomplices.

Using the information below, assign each crook to his henchman.

In March, Sylvius, Greystone, Petrovich, and Jackwort met, and each came with his personal henchman, Bert, Hank, Eddy, and Sam.

In May, it was Darius, Petrovich, Harvey, and Sylvius who got together, and they were with Hank, Ned, Sam, and Ian.

In June, Sylvius, Angelini, Greystone, and Darius met up and came with Gus, Bert, Sam, and Ned.

Jot down the names of the henchmen of Greystone, Jackwort, Harvey, Darius, and Angelini, in that order. The first letters of their names spell the first word of the next stop on the map.

Clash of Opposites

"Count Sylvius is so fearful of being tricked, he always automatically says the opposite of what I say. In fact, his opposition is so systematic, that it is relatively easy to lead him to where I wish him to go, simply by stating the opposite!" Holmes explains to Watson.

Speaking of opposites, can you find the opposites of the words below? The first letter of these antonyms will spell out a word.

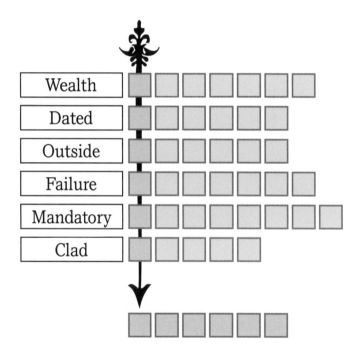

| Wealth |
| Dated |
| Outside |
| Failure |
| Mandatory |
| Clad |

The next destination on the map is a colloquial synonym for the word you just revealed.

Action!

"Holmes is rather a cerebral fellow," once said Scotland Yard Inspector Lestrade in a famous understatement. But at the end of the day, our detective can take quick and decisive action, like with the Mazarin Stone.

The photographer Muybridge, much to Holmes' delight, recently captured a sequence of quick actions. Below are the snapshots of the sequence showing someone doing a long jump. Place them in the right sequence and the letters underneath will form a word.

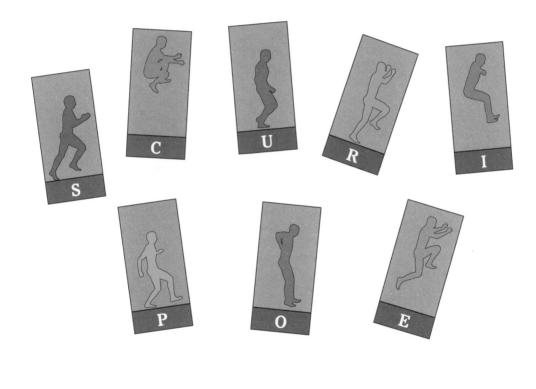

The word you have formed best
describes the object at the center of
your next location on the map.

Three Gentlemen

The prime minister, the home secretary, and Lord Cantlemere have arrived discreetly to Holmes' residence, trying to hide their identities, and before Holmes enters the room, they talk about their famous host's merits.

Each one, however, has a different opinion. Who is who and what are each of their opinions of Sherlock Holmes?

"You think that Sherlock Holmes will succeed, don't you?" says this gentleman.

"The home secretary isn't sure whether Holmes is up to it or not," says this gentleman.

"According to the prime minister, you, on the other hand, are convinced that he will fail," says this gentleman.

Gentlemen generally have one, but so do crooks. Count Sylvius' is at the next stop on the map.

Street Gangs

Elegant thieves, like Count Sylvius, rely on much less elegant street gangs to do their dirty work. Holmes has studied these ruffian gatherings and drawn up the diagram below.

Each big circle represent a gang with two to ten members (no two gangs have the same number). The arrows show how many members there are when two gangs join up (for example, when the East Siders join up with the Chapel Gang, there are ten of them). How many members are in each gang?

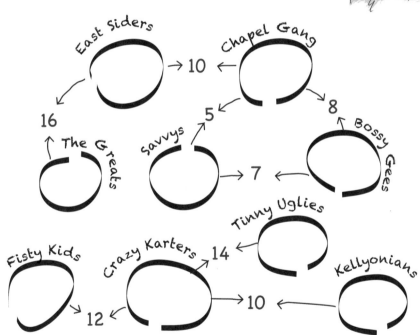

How many members are in The Greats and Tinny Uglies when they join up? That number is the next stop on the map.

Code of Conduct

Sherlock Holmes hastily scribbles two messages for Watson right before he leaves on his errand. They consist of two addresses, each one connected to a message. Both are of the utmost importance and must not fall into the wrong hands, so to be absolutely safe, Holmes has coded the messages with a system he shares with his friend.

Once deciphered, the first message reads "ADDRESS OF MURDERERS." What is the message with the second address?

> 136 Moorside Gardens
>
> ZAXQBMR LZ LRLCBLDO
>
> 35 Victoria Embankment
>
> ZJJZ YVZF
>
> TDQC QCB KLGFXB

On the map, go to
QZOHP JC VAYOZPN, which is
written with the second code.

Count Sylvius' Mustache

The most remarkable aspect of Count Sylvius is his formidable dark mustache. It's the first thing one sees, and only after does one notice the cruel, thin-lipped mouth and the long, curved nose that looks like the beak of an eagle. Holmes has noted that many a villain he has crossed had striking facial hair.

Each group of letters below can be rearranged to form the name of a style of facial hair—all, that is, except for one. Which one?

The odd word out is where you must go next on the map.

Being Murdered

"It's interesting, most interesting to see oneself being murdered," says Holmes. "Unforgettable." Not many people have such an opportunity, but Holmes clearly saw Count Sylvius ready to knock his brains out. Lucky for Holmes, the victim-to-be was his decoy. It was so unforgettable that Holmes can distinguish Count Sylvius' unique striking position from all the others.

Which position below is not part of a matching pair?

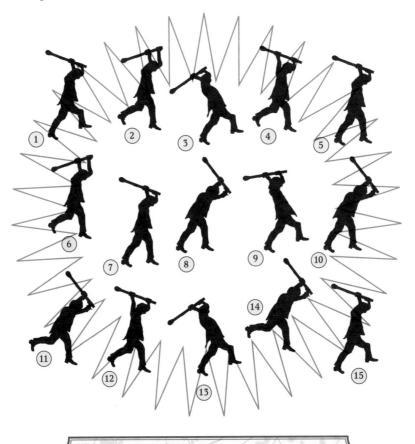

Multiply the number of the correct position by two for the next stop on the map.

Music for a While

Sherlock Holmes retires to his bedroom to play the violin, leaving Count Sylvius and Sam Merton to discuss how to deal with the situation. Holmes decides to play the daunting tune of Offenbach's barcarole, but his repertoire is large and he could well have played any one of the composers below.

    After placing each composer's name in the grid below, the letters in the gray squares can be arranged to form a word that indicates things are moving.

Berlioz
Bizet
Brahms
Corelli
Elgar
Glinka
Liszt
Mozart
Paganini
Schubert
Vivaldi
Ysaye

8   The word you have formed will help you find where to go on the map.

Four Famous Diamonds

"Count Sylvius could have stolen any one of these four famous diamonds, but because he's a connoisseur, he took the Mazarin Stone, by far the most precious one of the lot," comments Holmes while gazing at a reproduction of the four famous "yellow" diamonds.

"Which one is it?" asks Watson. "They all look alike to me . . ."

Instead of giving a straight answer, as is never Holmes' habit, this is what he says:

"If the East Star is not diamond 1, then it must be diamond 2.
"If diamond 2 is not the East Star, then diamond 4 is not the Karloff.
"If diamond 3 is not the East Star, then 2 is the Yellow Empress.
"The Mazarin Stone is, of course, one of the four."

Can you give each diamond its name?

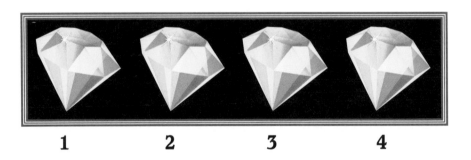

1   **2**   **3**   **4**

> An old woman on the map
> shows you where you
> must go next.

A Grumpy Visitor

Lord Cantlemere comes to see Holmes just to rant over what he assumes must be the detective's inevitable failure. Since the police have been unable to recoup the precious Mazarin Stone, he thinks the self-appointed detective, Holmes, can certainly do no better. However, his lordship lacks curiosity. If only he would consider the small, lettered cubes on the table, he might change his mind.

The seven cubes are identical. Can you determine what word would appear if he were to turn around each cube below so that the letter underneath appears on top?

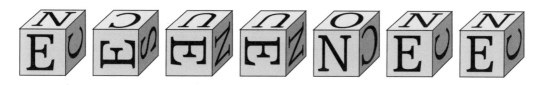

And with this word, our adventure comes to an end! Now you can find the first hidden word in the Sherlock Challenge.

CHAPTER 2
Wisteria Lodge

Alfred Hitchcock's remark "The better the villain, the better the picture" applies remarkably well to "The Adventure of Wisteria Lodge." Don Murillo, the Tiger of San Pedro, with his dark, deep-set brooding eyes, great bunched black eyebrows, and parchment face, is a remarkable villain. The deposed dictator, who imposes his will ruthlessly on all those around him, makes for a wonderfully powerful story. The villain is exceptional, but so is the policeman. Sherlock Holmes, who so often works with incompetent and suspicious police officers, finds in Inspector Baynes a notable exception. This inspector takes many shrewd initiatives, and his intuition is repeatedly praised by Sherlock Holmes.

This combination of a very bad baddy and an intelligent cop makes for a story in which Sherlock Holmes has to sharpen his wits to solve the successive mysteries, just as you will have to be on your toes to solve the following puzzles.

As explained in the introduction, use the map on pages 38–39 as a travel map. It will be essential to guide you through the strange places and events of this story to the final solving of the case.

Start with the first puzzle on page 40. Once you have solved it, follow the clue in the box at the bottom of the page to find your next destination on the map. This location comes with a number that gives you the number of the next puzzle you need to solve. Continue in this way, going back and forth, from puzzle to map, until you reach the last puzzle of the adventure. Have fun on your journey!

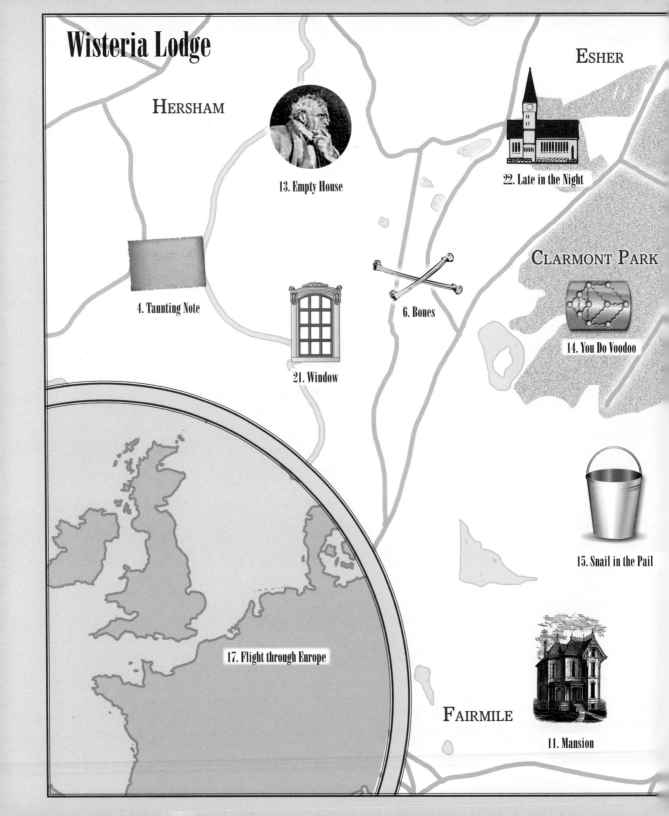

Wisteria Lodge

HERSHAM

ESHER

13. Empty House

22. Late in the Night

CLARMONT PARK

4. Taunting Note

21. Window

6. Bones

14. You Do Voodoo

15. Snail in the Pail

17. Flight through Europe

FAIRMILE

11. Mansion

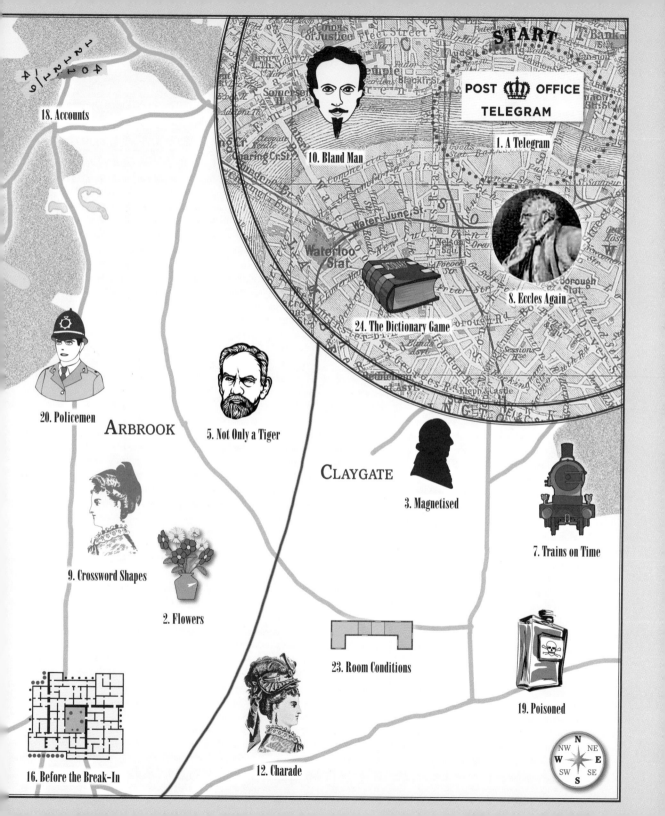

START

POST 👑 OFFICE
TELEGRAM

1. A Telegram

10. Bland Man

18. Accounts

8. Eccles Again

24. The Dictionary Game

20. Policemen

ARBROOK

5. Not Only a Tiger

CLAYGATE

3. Magnetised

7. Trains on Time

9. Crossword Shapes

2. Flowers

23. Room Conditions

19. Poisoned

16. Before the Break-In

12. Charade

A Telegram

A telegram arrives for Holmes, announcing the beginning of a new adventure. Luckily, the text of that telegram is in better shape than the one below. In this one, the words are in the wrong order, except for the first word. Watson can easily figure out the correct order, for the message is what Holmes says to many of his visitors when they try to tell him their story, and their thoughts become jumbled because they are tormented and scared.

Can you place the words of the telegram in the correct order?

POST 👑 OFFICE

TELEGRAM

Central Baker Street

PLEASE   AND   THOUGHTS

EVENTS   ARRANGE   KNOW   COMMA

LET   ME   HAVE   SENT

YOU   STOP   WHAT   HERE   YOUR

Once the telegram is in the right order, place BL before the sixth word. The new word tells you where to go on the map.

2
Flowers

To send her secret messages, Miss Burnet hides them in bouquets of flowers, but as an extra precaution, the flowers must correspond to a pre-established schedule that depends on the day of the week:

- On Mondays and Wednesdays, the bouquet must have four of the same flowers.
- On Tuesdays and Mondays, the bouquet must have at least one blue flower.
- On Wednesdays, the bouquet must have three or four different types of flowers.
- On Thursdays and Tuesdays, the bouquet must have three or more yellow flowers.
- On Fridays, the bouquet must have at least two white flowers.

For each bouquet below, find the corresponding day of the week for its message.

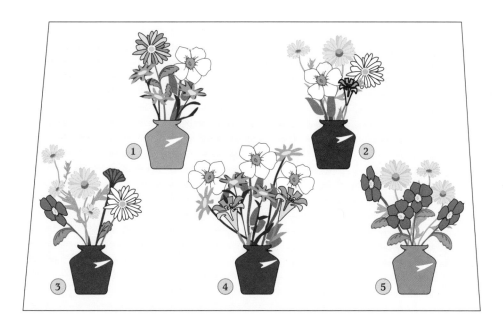

Go southwest on the map
in order to reach
your next stop.

Magnetised

Sherlock Holmes gives Watson a quick description of the people who live at High Gable. "There is Mr. Henderson, the owner, and the people who are magnetized by his personality: Mr. Lucas, his assistant; Eliza and Gladys, his daughters; and Miss Burnet, his daughters' governess."

"And how old are they?" asks Watson, not realizing what he is getting himself into. Below is Holmes' answer. Can you help Watson figure out everyone's age?

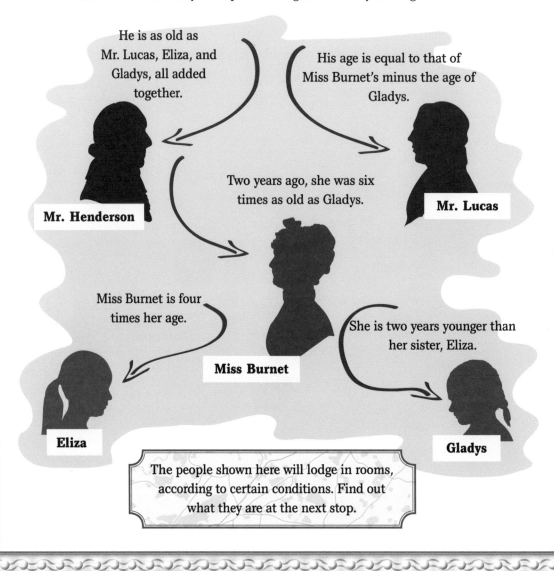

He is as old as Mr. Lucas, Eliza, and Gladys, all added together.

His age is equal to that of Miss Burnet's minus the age of Gladys.

Two years ago, she was six times as old as Gladys.

Mr. Henderson

Mr. Lucas

Miss Burnet is four times her age.

She is two years younger than her sister, Eliza.

Miss Burnet

Eliza

Gladys

The people shown here will lodge in rooms, according to certain conditions. Find out what they are at the next stop.

When Inspector Baynes shows Holmes a cryptic note he has just found in the fireplace at Wisteria Lodge, Watson is confident that his friend will discover its secret meaning. He remembers many an occasion when Holmes made sense of the most obscure texts.

For example, there was the time when a famous bank robber sent him a taunting note just before fleeing the country—or more precisely, just before Holmes had him arrested as he was about to step onto his private yacht.

Are you as quick-witted as our detective, who immediately spots his name in the note below? What does the message say?

YB HTT EMIY EUO

EDICHPRE HTSI OHMLSE

WILIB LF ERA WAYA

NEOJIYGN YM LI-

LOGTTNE OFTRNUSE

On the map, go to AMSNOIN,
written in the same code.

Not Only a Tiger

"Did you know, Watson," asks Sherlock Holmes, "that Don Murillo is not only known as the Tiger of San Pedro? His friends and foes also compare him to other animals. It's strange that such an unpleasant character should be compared to creatures not nearly as dangerous as he is."

Fill in the grid below, using the clues provided, to discover three of these animals in the white columns.

W	I	P		R	Manner of speaking
P	T	I		N	Pertaining to the Delphian priestess
D	R	N		E	Throw into confusion
A	G	I		Y	Without equanimity
T	C	L		R	Challenger on the field

Despite a few missing vowels, you can find
the name of your next stop:

P - L - C - M - N

Bones

"Well, well, well," mumbles Inspector Bayne, after making yet another sinister discovery. "Bones, bones, bones," he continues, as if everything needs to be repeated three times. He has just fallen upon a pile of bones carefully stacked one on top of another. "Why do you think that one's got a label attached to it?" he asks Sherlock Holmes.

"No idea," replies Holmes, candidly. "I wonder, Watson, how many bones have to be removed before one can grab the one with the label attached to it?"

What do you think? Of course, things have to be done neatly, without shifting any other bones out of place.

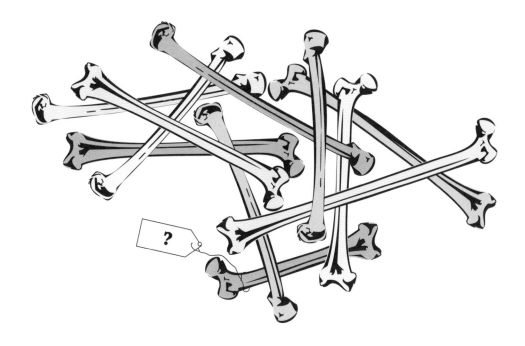

Three times the number
of removed bones is your next destination
on the map.

Trains on Time

Aplainclothes policeman was on watch at the railway station for just under twenty-four hours before Miss Burnet broke away from her captor, so he can answer Sherlock Holmes' questions.

"Only six trains for London have stopped at the station since I've been here. They left regularly, with the same interval between trains. And these are the times the trains left the station on my watch. Miss Burnet managed to escape from the last train that left. Luckily it was during the day, so she could see where she was going."

According to the clocks below, what time did Miss Burnet's train leave the station?

An anagram of POSEIDON indicates where
you should go to next
on the map.

Eccles Again

Watson has watched Holmes untangle the complex threads of the strange events at Wisteria Lodge, but there remains one point that he still does not grasp. "What," the doctor asks Holmes, "was the part played by Mr. Scott Eccles? How did this perfectly respectable Englishman come to be implicated in this sinister adventure?"

"Oh, he had a very precise role, I assure you," confirms Holmes. "Unwittingly, of course. The poor man is much too straightforward to realize that he was being used. But the end of one thing is the beginning of the next . . . "

Precisely. In the grid below, the missing last letters of the five-letter words on the left are also the first letters of the five-letter words on the right. Decipher these missing letters, and they will spell out Eccles' part in the story.

B	R	I	E			E	M	U	R
P	A	N	D			P	A	R	T
E	A	S	E			E	G	A	L
A	L	I	A			E	N	S	E
S	E	R	I			V	E	R	Y
T	I	B	I			F	T	E	R
T	I	D	A			A	I	T	Y
C	O	A	T			S	S	U	E
B	L	U	R			E	E	C	H
C	H	I	L			O	D	I	N

The grid contains another clue that indicates where you go next on the map.
(Hint: The spelling is British in style.)

Crossword Shapes

While playing word games with the young daughters of Mr. Henderson, Miss Burnet only has one thought on her mind. Once the governess has puzzled out this crossword-type puzzle, where each letter is replaced by a shape, she is able to spell out what is on her mind by using those same shapes.

Figure out the words in the puzzle to discover the word on Miss Burnet's mind, and as Sherlock will soon establish, the motive for her actions.

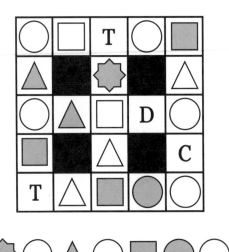

 5 The down word in the center takes you to your next stop on the map.

Bland Man

Sherlock Holmes is intrigued. What has come upon Mr. Aloysius Garcia, an affable and witty man-about-town, to invite for the weekend such a bland and insignificant fellow as Mr. Scott Eccles? Soon, our detective understands that it is precisely this blandness that Garcia is after.

"Looks just like anyone else" describes Eccles physically. In fact, you can only recognize him among the police facial composites below because he is the only one who has no distinctive feature. Every feature of his face can be found in at least one other portrait. Which one is Eccles?

Twice the number of the answer,
plus four, is the next destination
on the map.

Man and Mansion

The message found near the grate of the fireplace contains enough details for Sherlock Holmes to conclude that it it is about an appointment at a large stately home not far from Wisteria Lodge. Looking at the list of nearby homes, Holmes is struck by a correspondence between the names of the homes and their owners.

"It is not necessarily the home we are looking for," says Holmes, "but have you noticed, Watson, that the names of the owners and the names of the houses they live in all have a point in common except for one of them?"

Can you discern which one is the odd pair out?

Lord Harringby
- Nether Wessling

Douglass Fairford
- Oxshott Towers

Sir Clive Hammersmith
- Old Fatham Hall

Reverend Joshua Steel
- Huffington Manor

Mr. James Baker-Williams
- Ammonite Mansion

Robby McNethers
- Accadian Steps

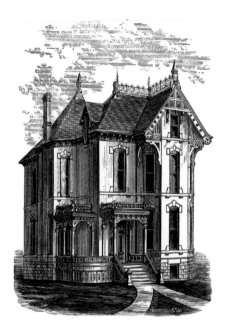

It's an essential part of a house for bringing in light and seeing out. It is also the word for your next stop on the map.

Charade

iss Burnet keeps her young wards entertained with many different games. The young ladies are particularly fond of the one they call Letter Charades:

My first letter is in PERJURED, CONJUROR, and ADJACENT.

My second letter is in JAUNTING, LEAKAGE, and HIJACK.

My third letter is in REACTION, FENCING, and ACROBATS.

My fourth letter is in RACKETEER, TACKLING, and DISLIKE.

My fifth letter is in CARETAKER, DAINTILY, and BACKDOOR.

My sixth letter is in POLLUTED, CHEWABLE, and BLOWUP.

And my whole is a name I would apply to someone I can think of and whom I don't much like!

> The number of your next destination on the map is in 45721 and also in 93280.

Empty House

When Scott Eccles awoke at Wisteria Lodge, he discovered, to his dismay, that everyone in the house had vanished. This unpleasant experience led Eccles to make three statements that he believes to be unquestionable truths:

- All the people living at Wisteria Lodge disappeared before breakfast.
- All foreigners are shady characters.
- All the people who left Wisteria Lodge before breakfast are foreigners.

And upon such sound premises, Eccles reached the following conclusions:

　　　　　1. All foreigners left before breakfast.

　　　　　2. All shady characters are foreigners.

　　　　　3. All the people who disappeared before breakfast live at Wisteria Lodge.

　　　　　4. All the people living at Wisteria Lodge are shady characters.

　　　　　Even if we don't agree with Eccles' opinions, which of his four conclusions are firmly based on his initial premises?

Add together the numbers of the statements that are true and go to that number on the map.

You Do Voodoo

The strange and morbid remains that the police found in Wisteria Lodge are finally explained by Sherlock Holmes. As he recounts later to Watson, one of the servants and accomplices of Mr. Aloysius Garcia practices a strange form of voodoo.

This little plaque found on the premises confirms the fact. How many different ways can you spell the word "voodoo," going from one letter to the next, only if they are connected, and never passing over the same letter twice?

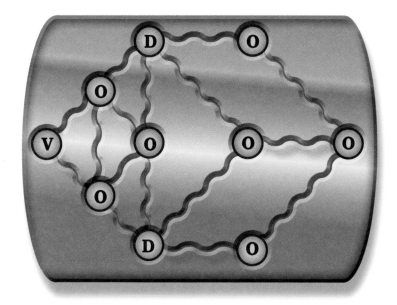

Twice the number of spelling "routes" takes you
to the next stop on the map.

Snail in the Pail

"Come and have a look at this!" cries out Inspector Baynes, who is standing next to an old bucket. Holmes and Watson look into the zinc pail and see a strange and sinister assortment of animal and insect remains.

"There's only one plant," comments Holmes, quite unruffled.

To spare you such an unpleasant sight, everything found in the bucket has been replaced by anagrams of their names. What is the plant Holmes observed?

throne

players

sneak

raptor

nails

totorise

looped

Along the same vein as this puzzle, NESBO
will show you where to go
on the map.

Watson is not particularly keen about Holmes' suggestion of breaking in to High Gable, but he goes along with it as an act of loyalty to his old friend. The house, however, has a maze of little rooms, and before taking action, they must plan their route.

They should, of course, avoid entering rooms where other members of the household might be sleeping. These are indicated with exclamation marks in the floor plan below. How should they proceed from the arrow to the room marked with an X?

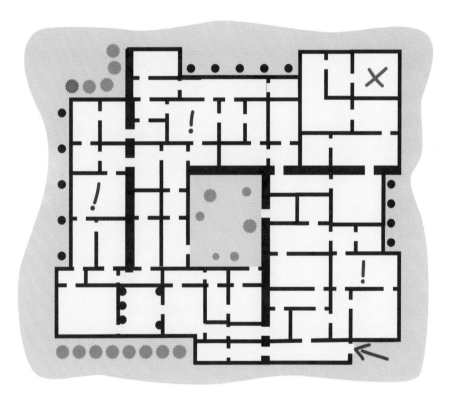

Words and shapes are to be found at your next destination.

17
Flight through Europe

Shortly after Holmes' investigation, the Tiger of San Pedro fled the country, and then continued fleeing from one country to the next until he met his fate. His first destination was France. He then went from one country to the next, following a strange superstition: his country of departure and his country of arrival must have three letters in common, no more, no less.

What was the last country of his erratic escape?

The vowel absent in the countries above appears four times in a word in the title of the next destination.

Accounts

The police continue checking through Mr. Aloysius Garcia's house and find in a wastepaper basket scraps of paper that look like torn-up accounts. They set aside the scraps, which appear to show sums paid as corruption money to various individuals.

"It would be of the greatest use," says Holmes, "if we could establish exactly what sums were lavished upon whom."

Put together the strips of paper below to find out the amounts received by each person on the list.

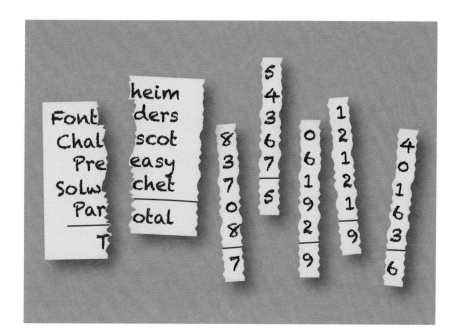

This story began with Mr. Scott Eccles, and there he is again at your next stop on the map.

Poisoned

Poor Miss Burnet has not only been held captive, but she also been given a slow-working poison. This causes her to be very weak, and also confuses her mind. In a strange, delirious fashion, she recites quotations on a subject much on her mind: freedom.

But the poison makes her so confused that two pairs of words are switched around in each quotation. Holmes easily puts things straight in his mind. Can you?

Who chains his mocks free not be will.

Free a better king than a bird in captivity.

Captivity is better in work, and be free than to be fed to it.

Others who deny themselves to those deserve it not for freedom.

Chains are not drag who free their they behind them.

A wild beast awaits you at your next stop
on the map.

Policemen on the Watch

"To make sure those villains don't get away, I'd like to place a policeman at every intersection," says Inspector Baynes. "However, I don't want to dispose that many officers."

"If you use only three, you can have adequate surveillance of all the roads on the map," comments Holmes.

At which numbered locations below should Inspector Baynes position his three officers?

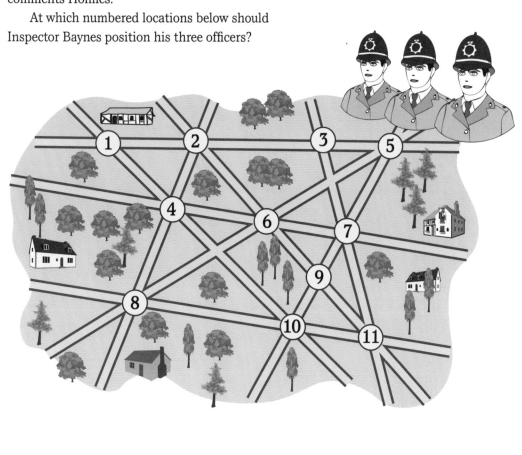

 The sum of the numbers of the three locations minus three is the number of the next stop on the map.

The Face in the Window

Constable Walters has had the fright of his life. There glaring at him through the window was the scariest face he could ever imagine. When pressed to describe it, he is so upset that he gives incoherent information.

With the help of Holmes' careful questioning and Watson's calming presence, a relatively precise picture of the face is sketched. It looks like the face that appears twice in the window below. Can you find the identical pair?

If A=1 and B=2, and so on, then the numerical values of the letters of the two faces added together give the number of the next stop.

Late in the Night

"**E**stablishing the precise time of an incident can be quite tricky, Watson," comments Sherlock Holmes, after hearing Mr. Scott Eccles' account of his stay at Wisteria Lodge.

At what time did Mr. Aloysius Garcia really call upon Eccles during the night?

During the night, Garcia tells Eccles that it is one o'clock in the morning.

But according to Eccles' watch, it is fifty minutes earlier.

The next morning, Eccles sees that his watch is fifteen minutes fast, compared to the church clock.

But a young lady tells him that the church clock is running ten minutes late.

When Scott Eccles awakes, the house is empty, and that's where you should go to on the map.

Room Conditions

Mr. Henderson, Mr. Lucas, Miss Burnet, and the two girls have settled in their rooms for the time being. Holmes has asked a few questions, here and there, to find out who is in which room, and he has reached the following conclusions:

- If Mr. Henderson is in an orange room, then Miss Burnet's room has three windows.
- If the girls have a room with a window looking southward, then Mr. Lucas is in a green room.
- If Miss Burnet's room has three windows, so does Mr. Lucas'.
- If Mr. Henderson is in a green room, then the girls are also in a green room.
- If Miss Burnet and the girls are next to each other, then Mr. Lucas is in an orange room.

So, who is in which room?

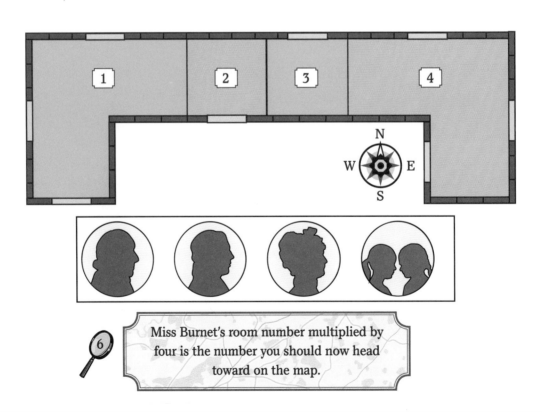

Miss Burnet's room number multiplied by four is the number you should now head toward on the map.

"How do you define the word 'grotesque'?" Sherlock Holmes asked Watson at the beginning of this adventure, and concludes, "As I have had occasion to remark, there is but one step from the grotesque to the horrible." Holmes is someone who likes words. He uses them with care and precision. Occasionally, he plays the Dictionary Game with Watson, with the assistance of Dr. Johnson.

"The following words apply rather well to that nasty character, Don Murillo," says Holmes. "Can you match Samuel Johnson's dictionary definition for each word?"

Boarish
Corrupt
Covetous
Ill-natured
Mortiferous
Noxious
Rapacious
Tyrannical

1. Not wanting kindness or goodwill
2. Fatal, deadly, destructive
3. Cruel, despotic
4. Given to plundering, seizing by violence
5. Swinish, brutal, cruel
6. Hurtful, harmful, destructive, pernicious
7. Inordinately eager for money
8. Without integrity, tainted with wickedness

You have now arrived at what can be defined as "the final part of something." Find the second hidden word in the Sherlock Challenge.

CHAPTER 3
The Second Stain

"The Adventure of the Second Stain," according to its narrator, Dr. Watson, is "the most important international case" that Sherlock Holmes has ever been called upon to handle. The story, set toward the end of the nineteenth century, gives us a glimpse into pre–World War I European politics. A letter written by an irresponsible foreign potentate is so provocative that it could easily lead to a "great war." Thanks to the cautious and lucid action of the British prime minister, greatly helped by Sherlock Holmes, the conflict is avoided.

After the clear-sighted and somewhat prophetic introduction, the plot centers on Holmes' actions and brilliant deductions. For you, the stakes are not as high, but the challenge is as sharp, so will you be able to attain the great detective's high standards in solving these puzzles?

As explained in the introduction, use the map on pages 66–67 as a travel map. It will be essential to guide you through the strange places and events of this story to the final solving of the case.

Start with the first puzzle on page 68. Once you have solved it, follow the clue in the box at the bottom of the page to find your next destination on the map. This location comes with a number that gives you the number of the next puzzle you need to solve. Continue in this way, going back and forth, from puzzle to map, until you reach the last puzzle of the adventure. Have fun on your journey!

The Second Stain

START

1. Gobbledygook

12. Famly Tree

20. Shadow of a Crime

22. Carpet Symmetry

7. Duplicate Key

11. Stolen Letter

14. Coded Initials

15. Hunting

16. Lady Hilda

ROMAN

5. Roman Message

10. Culprit or Victim ?

18 Precious Letter

3. Penny Patience

2. Number Combination

9. The Valet's Alibi

13. Master Spies

19. Lady Visitor

21. Two Explanations

4 Changing Personality

23 Crazy Logic

6. Spies on a Train

8. Postage

24. To Conclude

17. Potentate

Gobbledygook

Whe n the prime minister comes to see Sherlock Holmes about the stolen letter, he speaks with caution, but in a straightforward manner. His foreign secretary, on the other hand, has a much more convoluted way of expressing himself, and Holmes is at pains not to blurt out, "Speak clearly, man! Say what you mean!"

Instead, he just sums up wryly in a few words what the politician has said at length. Which of Holmes' summaries below is the correct interpretation of each of the foreign secretary's convoluted statements?

If I may express my innermost, yet inflexible, sentiment on this delicate though paroxysmally important matter, I cannot but reprove the opposition to the anti abolish capital punishment movement.

So, you are in favor (1) / you are against (2) capital punishment.

I would readily make the deepest objection to those who query that the feasibility of the project rests upon sound arguments.

So you consider we can go ahead (1) / we must not go ahead (2) with this project.

Smith claimed (quite erroneously, in my opinion) that the negative results of the test as to the innocuous nature of the medicine were not inconclusive.

So you would (1) / user would not (2) trust this medicine.

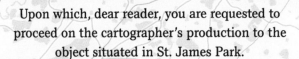

Upon which, dear reader, you are requested to proceed on the cartographer's production to the object situated in St. James Park.

2
Number Combination

Acavity is discovered under the carpet! What it contains will not be disclosed. But on many occasions, Holmes has had to figure out the number combinations for locks. On one occasion, he was lucky to find the (somewhat obscure) note that the owner had drawn up for the combination of his safe, in case he should forget it.

Below is the note. What is the number combination of the safe? To give you a head start over Holmes, it is useful to know that the combination is only comprised of the numbers 1 to 6.

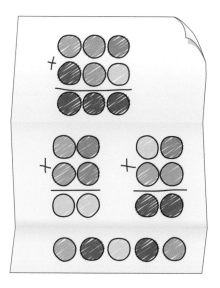

Add together the numbers of the combination
and the total will tell you the number to go to on
the map.

Penny Patience

After the prime minister's visit, Sherlock Holmes is totally absent, deep in thought and oblivious of his surroundings. Watson, patiently waiting for his friend to come back to the world, passes the time with a puzzle. He places pennies on a grid and challenges himself to end up with three coins on each row, on each column, and on the two main diagonals. To do this, he can only shift three coins, and each one only by one square, up, down, across, or diagonally.

Which coins should be moved and where?

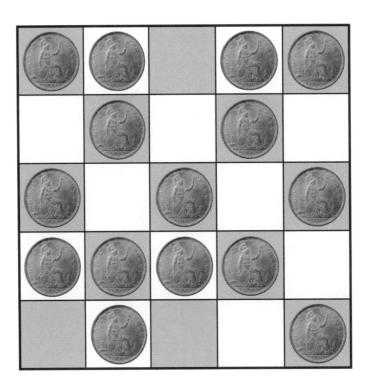

On the map, arm yourself with patience, and
go due west to your next destination.

4
Changing Personality

Inquiry into the life of the deceased spy has revealed that he was a shifty character in many aspects of his life.

"With people like him," sighs Watson, "you meet a charming, straightforward man of the world one moment, and a ruthless, scheming individual the next."

"Yes," agrees Holmes. "It's the same with words—one letter here, one letter there, and a word can change into another, quite contrary to the original."

With each of the examples below, take the first word, change one letter for another, then rearrange the letters to form another word. Continue in this way to arrive at the final word.

S	I	N	G	L	E
D	O	U	B	L	E

C	L	E	V	E	R
S	T	U	P	I	D

> Move on to the nearby lady
> along the English Channel.

Roman Message

After the murder of Eduardo Lucas, Sherlock Holmes contacted various informers. One of them brought him a book that he had found in the possession of a shady character lurking round the house of the victim.

"Well that's clearly a coded message, isn't it, Sherlock?" says Watson upon seeing the inscription in the book.

"Yes, you are right," answers the detective, "but contrarily to what you might think, it is not a numerical code. I guessed how to decipher it when I heard that it had most likely been written by that minor spy who calls himself Brutus the Roman."

Using Holmes' intel, can you decipher the message below?

Ƨ 50 50

100 Ƨ 50 1000

Ƨ 1000 1 500

1000 Ƨ 500

5 1 50 50 Ƨ

100 50 1 1000 Ƨ 10

50 Ƨ 500 1

1 50 500 Ƨ

1000 1 50 50

100 Ƨ 50 50

500 Ƨ 5 1 500

The next stop on the map gives two ways
of locking or unlocking.

Spies on a Train

Three counterspies, no less, had been following Eduardo Lucas as he traveled to Paris. They each sat in different carriages of the train in order to do their job without being spotted. Holmes questions the three counterspies, wanting to know the precise details as to where everyone was sitting in the train with forty-nine carriages.

"There were twice as many carriages ahead of mine as there were behind," states Harry, the first counterspy.

"There were three times as many carriages behind mine than there were in front," answers Dick, the second counterspy.

"I was between the two. There were five times as many carriages between mine and Harry's than between mine and Dick's," concludes Tom, the third counterspy.

"But where was Lucas?" asks Holmes dryly, on the verge of exasperation.

"I was two carriages closer to him than Dick," replies Tom, unruffled.

If the carriages are numbered from 1 to 49, from the beginning to the end of the train, in which carriage was Lucas?

The number of Dick's carriage minus four
gives you the number of the next destination
on the map.

Duplicate Key

Having had a duplicate of the safe key made, Lady Hilda wants to compare it with the original. She hastily grabs a great number of keys, but in her extreme state of nerves, she drops the duplicate among all the others. In her panicked state, she cannot find either the original or the duplicate. Can you help her find the two identical keys?

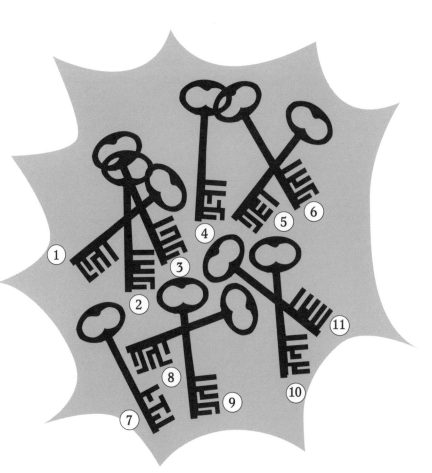

Add together the numbers of the two identical keys and go there on the map.

Postage

"Did he send it by mail?" jokes Watson, referring to the outrageous letter sent by a foreign potentate.

"He's too much of a miser for that!" joins in Sherlock, to the prime minister's surprise.

Had he sent it by mail, he should have placed stamps that totaled the value of 76 in his local currency. Which of the stamps below should he have used?

The Right honorable Lord Bellinger, Prime Minister of Great Britain

The number of your next destination on the map is the same as one of the correct stamps with the lowest value.

The Valet's Alibi

"**W**hen you arrived at the house, you checked your watch and it read twenty minutes past midnight. Is that correct?" questions Holmes.

"That's exactly right, sir," replies the valet who had discovered the murder the previous night. "But my watch runs a little fast," he adds.

"How fast?" asks Holmes.

"It gains two minutes every hour. But every morning, except for today, I set it on time at ten o'clock, along with the clock on the mantle."

"Why do you have to do that?" queries the detective.

"Mr. Lucas wants, err, I mean wanted his clocks to be on time, and this one loses three minutes every hour," says the valet.

The alibi can be a question of minutes, so Sherlock Holmes compares the time on the valet's watch with the clock on the mantle, both below.

What time did the valet come in last night?

Go to the number on the map that corresponds to 1600 hours on a twelve-hour clockface.

Culprit or Victim?

"The culprit was a victim," sighs Holmes to Watson's total incomprehension.

"The murderer?" asks Watson, incredulous.

"No, no, the person who stole the letter," clarifies Holmes.

"A victim? Really?" Watson has some difficulty following his friend's reasoning.

"And here's the reason," says Holmes, handing Watson a little puzzle in which the word to be found is the answer to the doctor's question.

Use the clues below to find the hidden word in the grid.

• The letter just between two identical letters.

• The letter just above an A, which is just above an M.

• The letter to the left of a K, which is to the left of a J.

• The letter below an N and just to the right of an L.

• The letter below an R, which is below a P.

• The letter to the left of an H and below an A.

• The letter that is above itself.

• The letter below an S and above a P.

• The letter next to an F, an M, and an N.

O	F	A	H	G	N	J	K
L	P	H	A	L	C	A	F
F	G	L	F	O	P	H	M
O	K	F	O	S	K	G	X
P	L	A	H	I	E	U	F
G	A	K	J	P	A	B	A
J	M	H	F	R	A	K	N
N	L	F	H	K	F	G	L

Move on to the engraving next to
the Houses of Parliament.

The Stolen Letter

Trelawney Hope stamps a little double symbol on every document he places in his safe. The double symbols have obscure meanings we need not go into here, but they all do appear with logical regularity.

An important letter that was placed in the safe has vanished. Holmes quickly guesses what symbols were stamped on it. Can you?

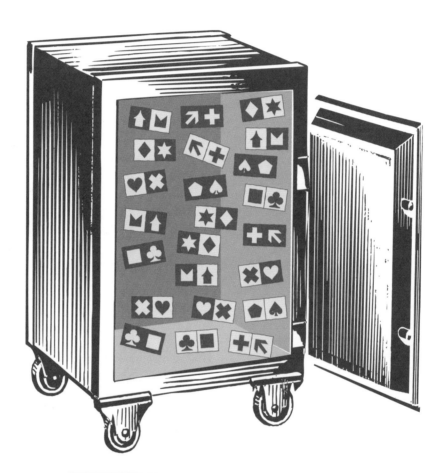

Find on the map a synonym for "ruler,"
"sovereign," and "overlord,"
and go there next.

Family Tree

When Lady Trelawney Hope is announced, Sherlock Holmes turns to his friend and says, "Quick, Watson, clue me in. Apart from being the wife of Trelawney Hope, who is she?"

"Lady Hilda Trelawney Hope," begins Watson, dutifully, "is the daughter of the Duke of Belminster, who is the grandson of that colorful figure known as Wallace the Valorous. This character had two sons, the Duke of Belminster's father and Nathaniel, who married Theresa Wetherby. Their son, Horace, is the father of our prime minister's wife. But to go back to Theresa Wetherby, she is the sister of the reputed patron of the arts, Clarissa Wetherby, and their father was that other legendary figure known as Cowardy Cuthbert. Well, be that as it may, Clarissa is the grandmother of Trelawney Hope, Lady Hilda's husband!"

Sherlock Holmes thinks about this for a moment and then asks, "So, am I right in saying that . . .

- Horace, the prime minister's father-in-law, is Lady Hilda's uncle?
- Trelawney Hope's great-grandfather was none other than Cowardy Cuthbert?
- Horace and the Duke of Belminster are cousins?
- Theresa Wetherby is the daughter of Cowardy Cuthbert and daughter-in-law of Wallace the Valorous?"

How many of Sherlock's statements are correct?

> The next destination on the map takes you to someone in this family tree.

Master Spies

Sherlock Holmes suspects that the stolen letter has been sold to one of the three most powerful international spies working in London: Oberstein, La Rothière, or Eduardo Lucas.

"Before dealing with these dodgy characters, it is worth getting to know them a little better. Do you know much about them, Watson?" asks Holmes.

"Nothing at all, I'm afraid to say," replies the doctor.

So, Holmes carries out a thorough inquiry on these master spies and comes up with the following conclusions:

- Between Eduardo Lucas and Oberstein, the less wealthy of the two is the oldest of the three.
- The one who pretends to be an art dealer is not as wealthy as the one who claims to be a journalist.
- Between Oberstein and La Rothière, the wealthier of the two is the oldest of the three.
- The supposed journalist is younger than the one who pretends to be a businessman.
- Between La Rothière and Eduardo Lucas, the elder of the two is the wealthiest of the three.

Can you discern the age, wealth status, and fake occupation of each spy?

The following destination is where one can toss a coin and play heads or tails.

Coded Initials

Sherlock Holmes questions, one after the other, all the policemen who have held watch at the murder scene. But because he is suspicious and cautious, he jots down their initials in his own personal code. Having found the man he was looking for, he writes down his full first name.

Watson, who is familiar with this code, can tell that the initials (in alphabetical order) are AL, AO, EA, LE, ND, NO, and OD.

What is the first name that is underlined below?

The next stop questions whether someone is
innocent or guilty.

Hunting

As Sherlock Holmes discovers, this hunting scene is in fact part of a complex memo. For some reason, Trelawney Hope is incapable of remembering the number combination of his safe, but he is also terrified by the idea that if he wrote that number down, someone could discover it. So his memo comes in two parts, this hunting scene and a note that reads as follows: The first number is twice the second, and the third is equal to the sum of the first two.

Can you figure out the five-figure combination using the hunting scene below?

The number of the third horse in the answer is also the number of the next destination on the map.

When Lady Trelawney Hope, the most lovely woman in London, enters Holmes' office, Watson is immediately subjugated. He cannot but admire the subtle, delicate charm and the beautiful coloring of her exquisite head. Of course, Holmes notices the effect she has on the doctor and as soon as she leaves, he turns to Watson and asks him . . .

Find out what Sherlock asks him in the grid below. Move adjacently from one letter to the next (not diagonally), starting in the upper left-hand corner and ending in the lower right-hand corner.

T	H	E	N	W	H	D	I
S	I	F	O	S	A	T	D
Y	X	A	I	T	E	H	T
O	E	S	R	A	L	A	D
U	E	N	T	W	E	R	Y
R	M	T	R	L	A	A	N
D	E	P	A	L	Y	W	T

5 Change the "E" to an "I" in the third word of the answer and go there next.

The letter that could bring war to Europe was written in a fit of anger by a foreign potentate. The prime minister is too discreet to name him directly, but Holmes finds a way of identifying the country he comes from.

Arrange the letters in the first circle below to form the name of a European city and jot down its first letter. Proceed in the same way with the second circle and jot down the second letter of the European city. Continue in this manner with the four remaining circles. The six selected letters will spell out the country where the politician is from.

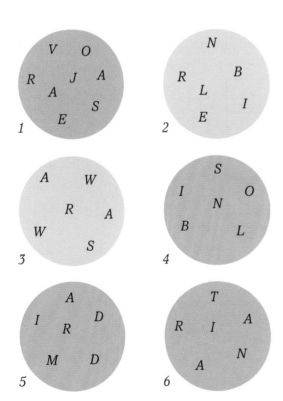

On the map, move just a little distance in a
northeasterly direction.

The Precious Letter

Trelawney Hope has brought his dispatch box to Sherlock Holmes. He opens it, empties it contents, and says, "See for yourself! I told you the letter isn't there!"

"I'd look a little closer if I were you," says Holmes. "If you were to pick up the letters, one by one, without ever taking one that is partially covered by another, you would pick up twice as many before you reached the letter as after the letter."

Which of the letters below is the precious letter?

Move on to your ultimate destination, number twenty-four.

The Lady Visitor

"Now, give this some thought before answering," says Holmes. "Your answer can implicate a very honorable lady. Do you recognize any of these women, and if so, can you tell me when you saw them?"

Holmes lays out five identity sketches before the policeman.

The policeman shifts from one leg to another a few times, and then after considerable hemming and hawing, he answers, "The lady who came on Monday, not the one in the striped dress, is between the ones who came on Tuesday and Wednesday. The one who came on Thursday is next to the one in the striped dress. The Friday visitor is not at either end, but the Wednesday visitor is."

Sherlock has the information he wants.

Can you tell who came on which day?

1	2	3	4	5

> The next stop on the map is where two
> gentlemen are in deep conversation near
> Waterloo Station.

⊷ 20 ⊷
The Shadow of a Crime

An avid collector of weapons of all ages, Eduardo Lucas had a panel where he displayed his finest pieces, and ironically, it was with one of these that he was savagely attacked.

"I see that the murderer left with the incriminating weapon," comments Holmes.

"Yes, there is one shape on the panel which doesn't have a corresponding weapon," confirms Watson.

Can you find it?

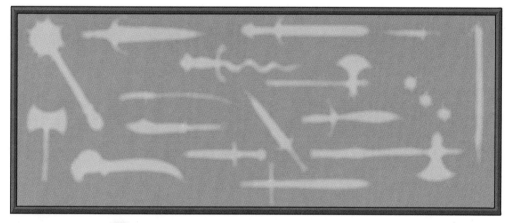

The next stop is by a tree that doesn't grow in
the woods.

"There are almost always two or more explanations to a problem," mumbles Holmes to himself, as he ponders what the prime minister has just said. "And sometimes," he adds, "both can be right."

"Just like this problem I'm puzzling over," comments Watson.

In the grid below, in every square with two letters, circle one of the letters to form words, like the solutions of a crossword puzzle. The letters not circled will form a second set of words that are equally valid.

A	O	W	L	E
T	M	P	E	R
A		A		E
D		O		A
M	A	R	I	S
P	E		T	T
I		D		E
E		K		T
R	R	S	I	S
T	A	A	P	N

Look on the map for Holmes and hidden capitals, which is where you must go next.

Carpet Symmetry

What strikes Holmes at first is, of course, the stain in the middle of the carpet, but the carpet itself also interests the detective.

"Have you noticed, Watson," says Holmes, "that the carpet is not symmetrical. There are ten details which differ from the overall symmetry."

Can you find them?

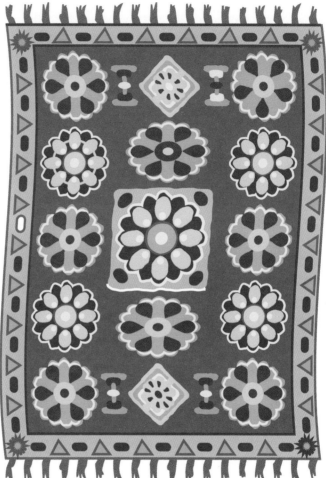

Find numerical circles on the map that combine to indicate your next stop.

Crazy Logic

"Mrs. Fournaye is not mentally sound, there's no doubt about it, and she has a logic of her own, which is sometimes quite difficult to follow," comments Holmes. "When I was questioning her the other day, she held the following discourse: 'I have noticed that amongst all the married men I have met, the ones who were jealous were liars and all the tenors were jealous. Some liars and all spies are unfaithful, but all tenors are faithful.'"

Had she known that her husband, the renowned tenor Mr. Eduardo Lucas, was also a spy, she would have realized that her reasoning was astray.

Which of the following statements about married men comply with the assumptions of Mrs. Fournaye?

1. A jealous man who is an unfaithful liar.
2. A liar who isn't jealous.
3. A spy who isn't a liar.
4. A tenor who does not lie.
5. A man who is not a spy, not jealous, not a liar, but yet is unfaithful.
6. A faithful spy.

For the next destination on the map, look out for a rug.

To Conclude

Watson knows full well how the precious letter ended up in the dispatch box from which it had disapeared, but the official version of the incident is somewhat different.

In the grid below, decipher this version of events by placing the letters in the columns below the grid in the corresponding squares above. The difficulty is finding the right order. Black squares come between words.

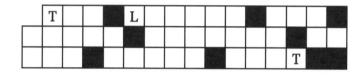

```
F A H E D E B E C A L O E A I T
W O S N N Ł E E R E R S S Ŧ S
  Ŧ U     V T T   U   W
```

This white lie, invented generously by Holmes, brings the story to its conclusion. Now it's time to find the third hidden word in the Sherlock Challenge.

CHAPTER 4
The Reigate Puzzle

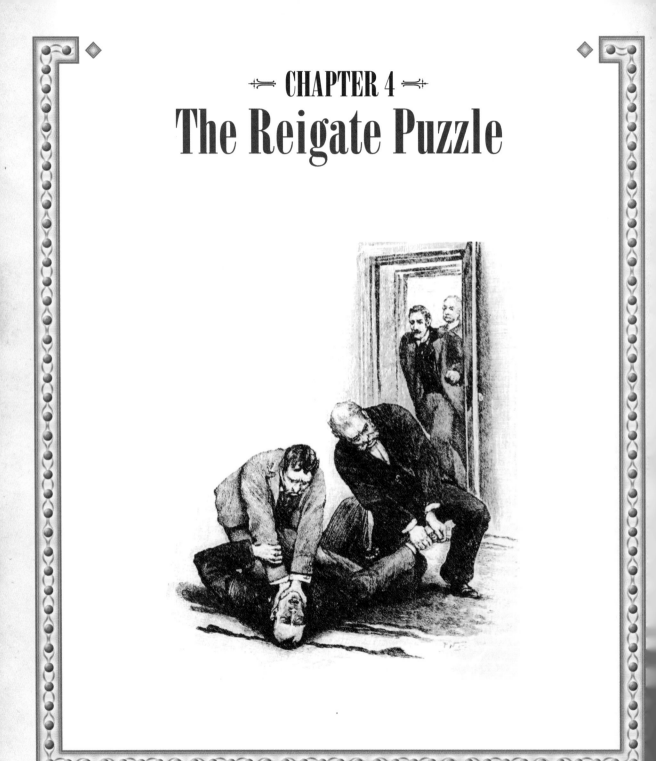

"The Adventure of the Reigate Puzzle," also known as "The Adventure of the Reigate Squires," begins with Sherlock Holmes recovering from nervous exhaustion in central France. This ailment is crucial to the story, not because Holmes is in any way diminished, but because on several occasions, he plays on it. At one point, he appears to faint in order to stop some vital information from being revealed. Another time, he gets his facts wrong, but again, this is intentional.

As it happens, the challenge of solving a murder is the best remedy for Holmes. He finds new and unsuspected resources of energy as the case progresses, and he gets to explore a whole aspect of criminology that he had neglected for a long time: the analysis of handwriting. The written word points to who is guilty, opening a window into their character and their intentions. Even though Holmes is in a weakened state, he's still sharp as a tack, making your attempt at solving these puzzles a challenge.

As explained in the introduction, use the map on pages 94-95 as a travel map. It will be essential to guide you through the strange places and events of this story to the final solving of the case.

Start with the first puzzle on page 96. Once you have solved it, follow the clue in the box at the bottom of the page to find your next destination on the map. This location comes with a number that gives you the number of the next puzzle you need to solve. Continue in this way, going back and forth, from puzzle to map, until you reach the last puzzle of the adventure. Have fun on your journey!

The Reigate Puzzle

WESTHUMBLE

7. Family Claims

5. Gap in the Wall

11. Wooden Blocks

15. Scrap of Paper

8. Light Lock

BUCKLAND

3. Lintel

REIGATE

12. Murder

18. Handwriting

21. Typo

16. Archery

LEIGH

17. Sandwich

22. Maze

19. Watson's Word

9. Diversion

14. Cracked Crockery

4. Killers

MERSTHAM

10. House to House

2. Bullets

23. Domestic Staff

REDHILL

13. House Plans

START

20. Robbery!

6. Word Wheels

1. Solitaire

SALFORDS

24. Chess Challenge

N
NW · NE
W · E
SW · SE
S

Solitaire

Exhausted after too much mental exertion, Holmes agrees to rest at the home of one of Watson's friends. While there, he is to stay calm and keep his mind at rest, but of course, such a lively intellect cannot remain passive, even at the best of doctor's orders. Under the pretense of playing solitaire, Holmes sets himself various challenges.

For this challenge, he deals five random playing cards and challenges himself to find a reason for each card to be the odd one out. For some, the answer is obvious, less so for a few others, and possibly a stretch for the rest.

Can you come up with good reasons for each card being "the odd one out"?

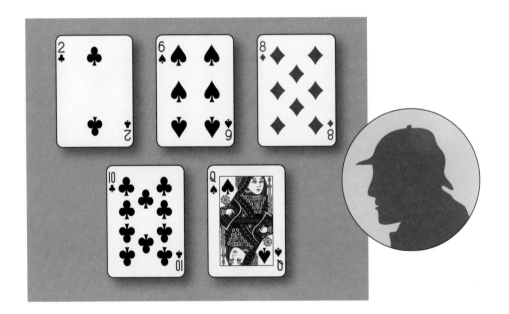

Using the numbers on the cards above, add together the clubs, divide by the six of spades, and then add half the diamonds for the number on the map.

2
Bullets

Holmes, in many ways, can be considered to be a precursor of modern investigative methods. When a suspect's gun is seized, he immediately realizes that it is a precious piece of evidence. If the bullets it fires are deformed in a similar way to the bullet that was found in the victim, then the likelihood that it is the murder weapon is very high.

Find two identical bullets below, both deformed in the same way after having been fired by the same gun.

On the map, move due west to the closest destination.

The Battle on the Lintel

The door of the Cunninghams' house bears the name of the Battle of Malplaquet on the lintel. Upon seeing it, Holmes automatically mumbles the date of the battle.

"Do you know the date of all great British battles?" asks Watson, impressed.

"Most," acquiesces Holmes. "I have a little memorization trick . . .

"Malplaquet is 'onto several naughty nightingales.'

"For Agincourt, I use 'only fold once finished.'

"For Trafalgar, it's 'on either nifty finger.'

"And for the Battle of Shrewsbury, I use 'one fortunate National Theatre.' "

"What about the battle of San Romano?" asks Watson, thinking he would catch his friend with this conflict, famously illustrated by Uccello, but totally foreign to English history.

" 'Once for the twilight,' " replies Holmes without hesitation.

Can you figure out Holmes' mnemonic trick and come up with the dates of the battles?

> Using Holmes' memorization method, the number of the next stop on the map is "only silver."

4
Killers

Holmes realizes from personal experience that people who have killed once are always ready to do so again. It seems to be such a common occurence that the vocabulary surrounding killings and violent deaths in general is extremely abundant.

Here are a few such words and they all fit in the grid below: assassinate, carnages, crime, eliminate, execution, fell, gash, homicide, kill, liquidate, murderer, and slay.

Once you have placed all the words, the letters in the gray squares can be arranged to form a word describing the fate Sherlock narrowly escaped.

The title of the next stop refers to what killers put in their guns.

Gap in the Wall

According to Alec Cunningham, the man who shot the coachman ran out of the property, possibly slipping through the gap in the low wall. Holmes takes in all the details of the area—the greenery, the shrubs, the ditch, and the open wall—even to the point of noticing exactly the number of bricks that are missing.

How many bricks are needed to mend the wall below? Note that it has a particularly robust structure and is two bricks thick.

Once you know how many bricks are needed, divide the number by two, and then subtract three. This is the number of the next stop.

Word Wheels

D r. Watson looks after his illustrious patient and does his best to keep his mind busy, but as far away as possible from any criminal investigation. For this endeavor, he plays various games with Sherlock.

On this occasion, Watson asks him to complete each circle below with one letter in order to form a word related to a sound physical condition. This word can be read in either a clockwise or a counterclockwise direction, once you find the first letter of the word, which is placed in a different spot in the circle for each word. The nine missing letters, when placed in the correct order, will then form a word on the same theme. What is this word?

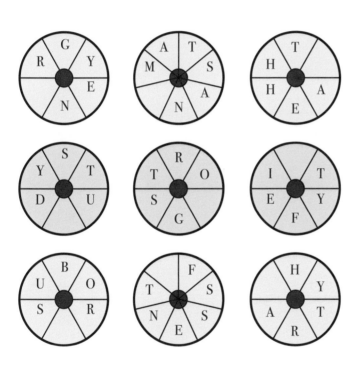

To find your next stop on the map,
go westward to the furniture.

Family Claims

The two wealthiest families of the region, the Actons and the Cunninghams, have been squabbling over property for years. Their lawyers have been having some difficulty in establishing not only what belongs to whom, but also who claims what.

After questioning some Acton family members, Holmes comes to the conclusion that each one says the truth on two counts, but lies (or shall we say is mistaken) on the third. With this information, the detective can establish the Acton family claims. Can you?

On this property, our family owns . . .

seven fields, four barns, and the house.

eight fields, four barns, and two ponds.

eight fields, three barns, and the house.

seven fields, one pond, and the woods.

the house, three barns, and the woods.

Twice the number of fields plus half the number of barns gives you the number of your next destination on the map.

8
Light Lock

A fter the arrest, policemen search the house and come upon a door with a complex safety mechanism, but after trying various combinations, the inspector has to call upon Holmes for help. The detective looks carefully at the odd setup and comes to the following conclusion: "To open the door, all the lights have to be switched off—"

"But that's the problem!" interjects the inspector. When I switch them around, others light up. I can't make heads or tails out of it."

"Indeed, it's tricky," concedes Holmes. "What you have to do is always simultaneously switch two switches that are next to each other."

With this precious help, how would you go about turning off all the lights?

Find little wooden cubes on the map, which correspond to your next destination.

Diversion

The investigation into the coachman's murder places Inspector Forrester in the center of attention. He enjoys this newfound importance and tends to talk too much. On this occasion, he almost gives away some vital evidence to the suspects. To avoid such a disastrous revelation, Sherlock Holmes sharply diverts the conversation by pretending to lose consciousness.

Everyone immediately flocks around the detective, describing his indisposition differently. Five of these descriptive words can be found in the clouds below. The first letter of each word is in the first cloud, the second letter in the next, and so on. Form the five words.

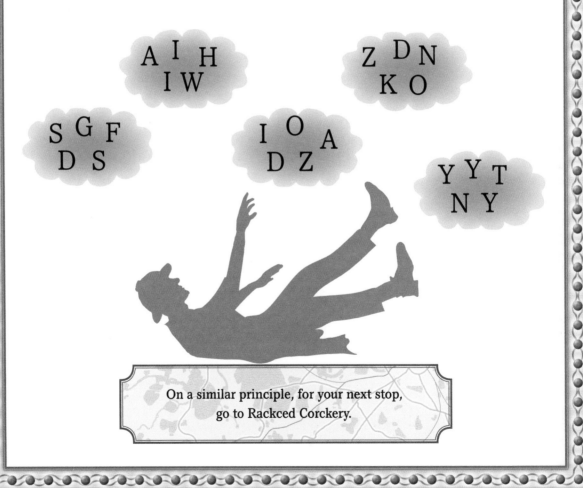

A I H
I W

Z D N
K O

S G F
D S

I O A
D Z

Y Y T
N Y

On a similar principle, for your next stop,
go to Rackced Corckery.

From House to House

Inspector Forrester has had a constable inquiring into the murdered coachman's movements the day before the crime.

"I've discovered," the inspector says to Holmes, "that the coachman, at one moment in the afternoon, went on a round of four houses in this district. After starting at one house, he walked to another house, and on to another, and then to a fourth one, before returning to the house he originally came from. He did this without passing by any other house."

"Indeed," replies Holmes, "with that information, I can find at least a dozen journeys just in this area. But every little bit helps."

Find twelve different journeys that form a loop passing by four houses (with the departure and arrival house counting as one house), without going back on one's steps.

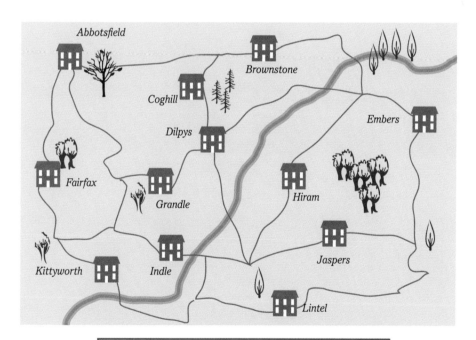

On the travel map, move to the destination with the same name as the house farthest south on the map above.

11
Wooden Blocks

"How on earth did you piece all that together?" asks Mr. Acton, impressed by Sherlock Holmes' explanations.

"Oh, often it's just a question of seeing things correctly," the famous detective replies modestly. "Look at these little blocks of wood, for instance," he adds, picking up various parts of an antique building set. "They all seem quite different, but it's just a question of how you look at things."

How many different structures are below?

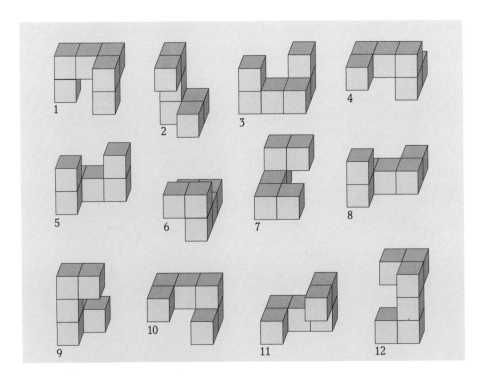

The total number of cubes in any three of these structures minus one will give you the number of your next destination on the map.

Holmes, Watson, and their hosts are quietly conversing when the peace is broken by shrill shouts announcing the murder of William Kirwan, the unfortunate coachman of a nearby household.

After the flurry has subsided, someone asks, "What were we talking about?" Indeed, can you figure out in the text below what object Holmes was describing in such detail?

MURDER!!!

MURDER!!!

MURDER!

MURDER!

This apparatus has only recently been patented in the United States of America, but I trust it will enter most of our homes before long. It comes in three parts. One which rests in the press with a little winding handle on the side and two parts which you can hold in either hand. In one of these you can talk while you take the other to your ear. This contraption allows you to converse with people who can be quite some distance away.

On the map, go in a northeasterly direction,
where you will find your next stop.

Before entering the Cunninghams' house, where Alec Cunningham witnessed the shooting of William Kirwan, Sherlock Holmes asks the inspector to explain the layout of the rooms.

"Oh, it's all pretty standard, you know," says the inspector. "Every window you can see from here belongs to a room. For instance, behind that window is old Mr. Cunningham's room, just above the library. Young Alec Cunningham's room is behind the window over there, with his private dressing room just next door. Then there's the room of Mr. Cunningham's manservant, which is just to the right of the study. There's also the maid, who has a room above the billiard room. When you enter through the main door, you enter a large hall with the drawing room on your left and the library on your right.

"Yes, it's a bit strange, but the billiard room and the dressing room are next to each other."

Sherlock Holmes immediately understands the layout of the house and can tell which room is behind which window. Can you?

Move on the map to the people who run the house.

Cracked Crockery

While visiting the rooms in the Cunninghams' home, Sherlock deliberately knocks over a low table on which there were plates and fruit. Two plates break and the fruit rolls all over the place. This is a perfect diversion for the detective to slip away unnoticed. Watson, who takes the blame for the incident, helps pick up the bits. He manages to find all the pieces of one plate, but search as he may, he cannot find the last part of the second plate.

Below are the fragments and two plates just like the ones that were broken. Is the missing bit from the green or blue plate?

On the map, to find your next stop,
just move straight east.

Scraps of Paper

Inspector Forrester shows Holmes a small piece of torn paper found between the finger and thumb of the murdered coachman. From this small scrap of paper, our detective gathers a wealth of unsuspected information.

Below, a number of words have been written on slips of paper that have then been torn in two. Find the pairs that go together to form twenty words. All are related in meaning, except for one. Find it!

ASSE · ENCO · VIEW · NTION
CONGR · SEM · ENCE · OSIUM
INTER · ASSO · ILY · EGATION
GATH · COU · MBLY · NION
APPOIN · CONVE · ERING · LAVE
CONFE · SYMP · UNTER · RESS
· CAU · INAR · TMENT
FAM · MEE · CUS
AUDI · RENCE
CONSU · CONG · CIATION · NCIL
REU · CONC · TING · LTATION

The odd word out gives you part of the name of your next destination.

5

Archery

The day before the crime, Alec Cunningham had held a private archery contest. The arrows are still in the targets when Sherlock Holmes comes round to check out the house.

"What were the scores?" asks Holmes genially.

"I had the top score, 78 points," boasts Cunningham. "My father's manservant scored 63 and my father 56."

"What did William Kirwan score?" asks Sherlock, deliberately, bringing the murdered coachman to the fore.

"That's his target on the side," replies Cunningham, adding, "you can work out the score for yourself."

And Sherlock promptly does.

What was the coachman's score? Each section gives a different number of points, which are not those used in official contests.

1 — The number of the next stop on the map is half the value of the blue sections on the targets above.

U pon seeing one of Mr. Acton's servants biting hungrily into a piece of meat between two hefty slices of bread, Holmes says jokingly to Watson, "Isn't that what is now called a 'sandwich'?"

"Indeed!" confirms Watson. "You know, there's a word game based on the same concept. The first word is like the top slice of bread, and the second word is like the bottom slice of bread. The last three letters of the first word are the first three letters of the second word, and the middle letters form another word, reading downwards, which is like the meat!"

Following the sandwich concept, what word is formed in the outlined center squares below?

T H R			E R S
R A M P			I C L E
J A V E			O C U T
M A J E			L I S H
A C R Y			E N C E
A N C I			I T L E
C A B B			N D A S

8

The end of "grandma" and the beginning of "Zelda" spell out the name of your next destination on the map.

The Handwriting Proof

This is not Sherlock Holmes' first time using handwriting analysis to solve a case. For a while, he was passionate about the matter and considered a number of minor cases, just to test his capacities in this field. On one occasion, a gentleman called George Fellows denied having written a recognition of debt. "Just look at the handwriting!" he claimed. "It's nothing like mine."

Holmes was called in to settle the matter. He asked George Fellows and five suspects to sign their names, and with this evidence he came to a surprising conclusion.

In your opinion, who wrote the note below?

George Fellows

Margaret Freize

Henry Markham-Sargent

Theresa Caltenborough

Adrian Buckley

Harold Shawnbush

I, the undersigned George Fellows, recognize that I owe three hundred and sixty-four pounds to Henry Markham-Sargent, who lent me the said sum on September the fourth eighteen eighty-four.

George Fellows

The next stop on the map also concerns a message, but it is typed or, shall we say, mistyped.

Watson's Word

W hen all is over, Sherlock Holmes reveals how he progressed toward resolving the case, and also admits that at times, he was using his ill condition to reach his ends.

While pondering this information, Watson invents this little puzzle. Adding a letter to the center of each star below will complete three words that can be read in the direction of their arrows. These five letters will then, in turn, form another word.

Can you figure out this word?

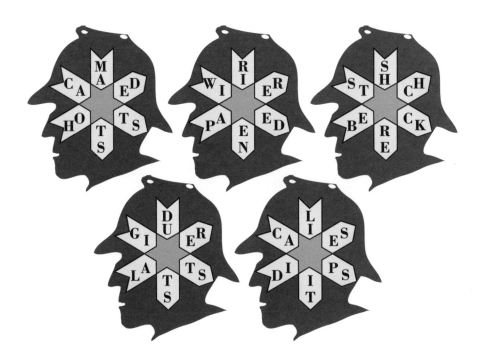

Go to the challenge usually played with a king, a
queen, bishops, and knights.

20
Robbery!

A house not far from where Holmes is staying has been robbed, but strangely, the thieves moved everything about and made a frightful mess without hardly taking anything. Sherlock immediately begins puzzling over this odd behavior, but Watson stops his friend before he gets carried away, reminding him that he is here to rest his mind.

Even though Holmes is not allowed to go further, you can still puzzle out what has been stolen. Among all the objects tidily placed at the top of the image below, which ones cannot be found in the pile below them?

Take the number of stolen objects, multiply it by four, and then go to that number on the map.

Typo

The note that was sent to the unfortunate coachman was a puzzle for Holmes in having to analyze the handwriting. A few years later, he will have to face a different challenge: typewritten letters. On one occasion, he comes upon a letter that has so many typing mistakes that he can hardly believe it. There is a wrong letter in every single word.

However, he realizes that there is a method to these typos—a hidden code!
This letter is below. Can you figure out the hidden message?

```
Deer Sin,

Coult ee arrrnge bo myet
somebhere clase co tke
sdation noxt weok?
R suggesk Seturday ay
twilve o'clonk.
World thet suid jou?
Sincarely yourr,
```

Fox youn nexx destinotion of thy mip,
gu tu Mouse Plant.

Maze

Delighted by the happy outcome of Sherlock Holmes' investigation, Mr. Acton invites the detective to his house and proudly shows him the maze he is having built in his garden.

"The idea is that one enters here and can leave through any of the three exits."

"To do that," says Holmes, "you must remove five blocks."

Which five blocks need to be removed so that anyone entering the maze at the top-left corner can leave through any of the exits at the other three corners?

Go east on the map in order to reach
your next stop.

Domestic Staff

A t one point during the investigation, Sherlock Holmes asks to see all the regular and occasional servants who work for the Cunninghams. As in most households of the time, there are many.

Perdita Horn, the housekeeper, is eager to meet the famous detective, and volunteers to introduce her colleagues who were present at the time.

"First of all, I must introduce you to Anthony Mason. He is our manservant, and, after me, the most important member of the domestic servants. And here we have his wife, Aida Mason, who acts as a maid. Then there is the footman who has recently joined the household, and is called, um, yes, Manuel Fox—that's right, isn't it? Good, and lastly, here is Terry Posher, who is—"

"Let me guess," interrupts Sherlock Holmes. "If he follows the rule that seems to govern the names around here, he must be . . ."

So, logically, how should Holmes finish his sentence? With . . .

the steward?

the valet?

the porter?

the gardener?

the butler?

On the map, all you need do is move directly
upward, where you will find
your next stop.

Chess Challenge

Having successfully solved the Reigate Puzzle, Sherlock Holmes returns quietly to his hosts and continues to activate his brain by puzzling over a chess problem of sorts.

"What ever is this chess disposition?" queries Watson upon seeing *three* white queens and no less than seventeen black pawns.

"It's a special Holmes puzzle," replies Sherlock with a mischievous smile. "I overcame two murderers, so I'm trying three queens! Can you place the three white queens on the board so that every single pawn is threatened with immediate capture?"

Remember, a queen can capture any other piece that is in a straight line, horizontally, vertically, or diagonally, however many squares away.

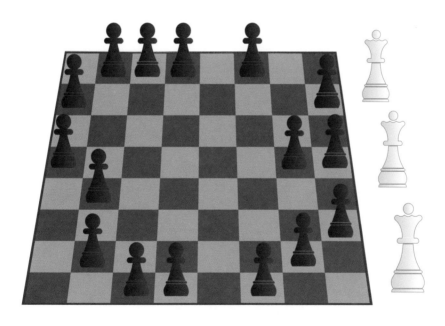

Here you arrive at the final stop of your journey. Now you can find the fourth hidden word in the Sherlock Challenge.

CHAPTER 5
The Greek Interpreter

In some stories, Sherlock Holmes is essentially a brain who puzzles things out without taking much part in the action; in others, he is an active element in revealing the truth. In "The Adventure of the Greek Interpreter," our detective has little part in unraveling the story, and even though he dashes about much of the time, he only has a minimal impact on the course of events. Nevertheless, Conan Doyle readers regularly classify this story among their favorites of his. The reason, no doubt, is the introduction of the wonderful, nonchalant character Mycroft, Holmes' older brother.

We also meet Mr. Melas, the interpreter of the story's title, who shows many qualities shared with Holmes, most notably, his faculty for getting information. In one scene, he has been kidnapped, but he manages to interrogate another character right in front of his captors without them realizing it. Your skill for discovering hidden information is one you will find most useful when solving the following puzzles.

As explained in the introduction, use the map on pages 122–123 as a travel map. It will be essential to guide you through the strange places and events of this story to the final solving of the case.

Start with the first puzzle on page 124. Once you have solved it, follow the clue in the box at the bottom of the page to find your next destination on the map. This location comes with a number that gives you the number of the next puzzle you need to solve. Continue in this way, going back and forth, from puzzle to map, until you reach the last puzzle of the adventure. Have fun on your journey!

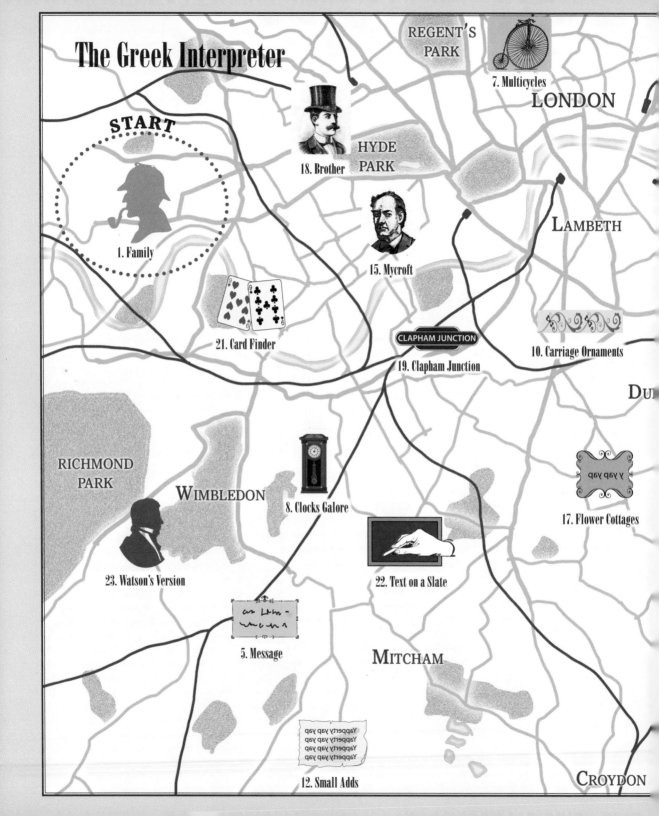

The Greek Interpreter

START

1. Family

REGENT'S PARK

7. Multicycles

LONDON

18. Brother

HYDE PARK

15. Mycroft

LAMBETH

21. Card Finder

CLAPHAM JUNCTION

19. Clapham Junction

10. Carriage Ornaments

DU

RICHMOND PARK

WIMBLEDON

8. Clocks Galore

17. Flower Cottages

23. Watson's Version

22. Text on a Slate

5. Message

MITCHAM

12. Small Adds

CROYDON

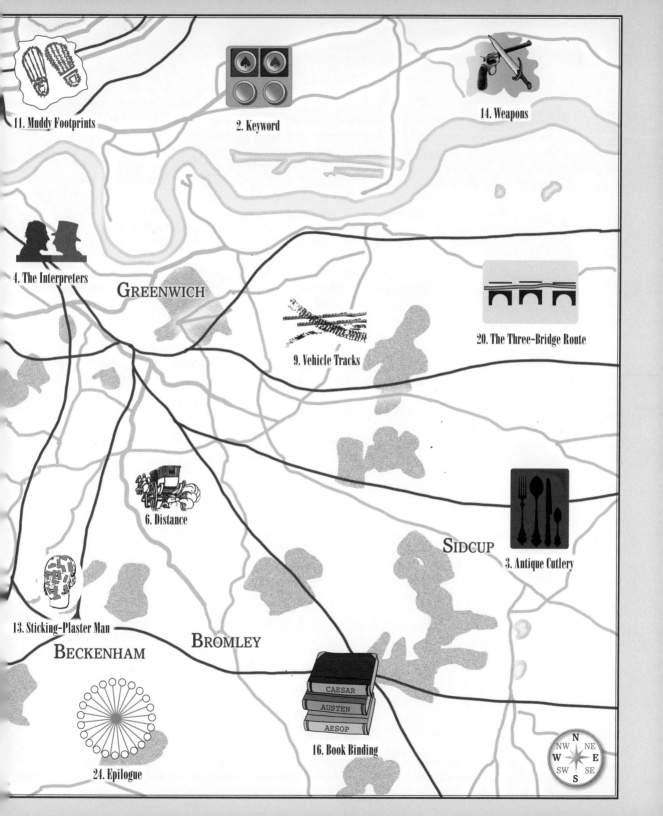

11. Muddy Footprints

2. Keyword

14. Weapons

4. The Interpreters

GREENWICH

9. Vehicle Tracks

20. The Three-Bridge Route

6. Distance

SIDCUP

3. Antique Cutlery

13. Sticking-Plaster Man

BROMLEY

BECKENHAM

CAESAR
AUSTEN
AESOP

16. Book Binding

24. Epilogue

NW N NE
W E
SW S SE

Family

At the beginning of this story, Watson discovers that Sherlock Holmes is not, as he had supposed, an orphan, but that he has a family: a grandmother, who is related to a famous French painter, and an older brother.

To celebrate this newfound family, find all the words related to families in the grid below. They are written in all directions, including diagonally. Words can also overlap.

ancestors
aunt
baby
birth
brood
brother
cast
clan
cozy
daughter
event

family
father
grandchildren
grandfather
grandmother
greatgrandfather
greataunt
heirs

husband
icon
kids
kinsmen
lineage
male
mother
name

nephew
niece
offspring
parent
pedigree
relation
roots
scions

second
cousin
siblings
sister
sons
strain
team
tribe
twins
uncle
wife
youngsters

F	G	R	A	N	D	M	O	T	H	E	R	E	T	N	E	R	A	P
A	S	R	I	E	H	E	S	P	E	D	I	G	R	E	E	B	D	N
M	T	O	E	M	L	N	I	E	C	E	C	A	S	T	S	O	E	O
I	R	O	N	A	L	C	S		O	E	T	N	O	R	S	F
L	A	T	M	N	T	R	T		N	N	O	R	D	D	T	F
Y	I	S	O	N	S	G	E		S	I	B	L	I	N	G	S
S	N	E	P	H	E	W	R		C	L	I	K	U	B	R	P
R	R	R	E	T	H	G	U	A	D	S	O	H	F	A	T	H	E	R
O	E				E	L	C	N	U	C	U					L	I
T	H			W	I	F	E	D	E	S			A	N
S	T			T	W	I	N	S	F	B				T	G
E	O	T	G	R	E	A	T	A	U	N	T	A	I	H	T	R	I	B
C	M	R	E	H	T	O	R	B	E	V	E	N	T	R	C	H	O	B
N	E	Y	O	U	N	G	S	T	E	R	S	D	R	H	T	O	N	A
A	T	E	A	M	N	I	S	U	O	C	D	N	O	C	E	S	Z	B
K	I	N	S	M	E	N	R	E	H	T	A	F	D	N	A	R	G	Y

The letters that don't belong to any word will repeat one of the given words. This word is the name of your next stop on the map.

Keyword

When Sherlock Holmes and Watson arrive at Scotland Yard, they find Inspector Gregson in a foul mood, glaring at a set of counters.

"It's these wretched counterfeit money producers," he grumbles. "They communicate by code and I can't figure out the keyword. I know that to start with, I must place these counters in the appropriate notch. Here's what it says: 'One club must be just between two hearts. Two spades are next to each other. No red sign should go in a red notch. The green heart is not next to a spade.' What do you make of that?"

After a moment's reflection, Sherlock manages to place the counters appropriately, much to the inspector's annoyance.

"No," the inspector grumbles, "you must turn them over so that the letters on the back appear. Holmes dutifully turns over the counters.

"You see!" says the inspector triumphantly. "It doesn't mean a thing!"

"It's a start," replies Holmes quietly. "How about . . . yes, how about using the first letter that follows the first letter alphabetically, the second letter that follows the second letter . . ."

Holmes is right. What is the keyword?

Front view

Back view

An anagram of the name of your next stop on the map is SNOW PEA.

Antique Cutlery

Once the Greek interpreter is taken somewhere safe, the police search around the house for clues as to where the kidnappers could have fled. Thus, they come upon these odd sets of cutlery with prices attached. What could it mean? Were the owners of the house implicated in some traffic of antiques?

"I wonder why there isn't a price on that middle one?" queries the inspector's assistant.

"Well, each piece of cutlery seems to have a set price, so it shouldn't be too hard to work out," comments Holmes.

Find the value of the set below without a price.

 Go downward and slightly to the left on the map,
stopping at the nearest destination.

The Interpreters

The Greek interpreter, Mr. Melas, is very precious, for he is the only person in London who can interpret directly from Greek into English. The only other solution, notes Sherlock, is to pass through four different interpreters (from Greek to language 1, then from language 1 to language 2, and so on).

Even finding a chain with only four interpreters isn't that easy. How would you go about it using the translators below?

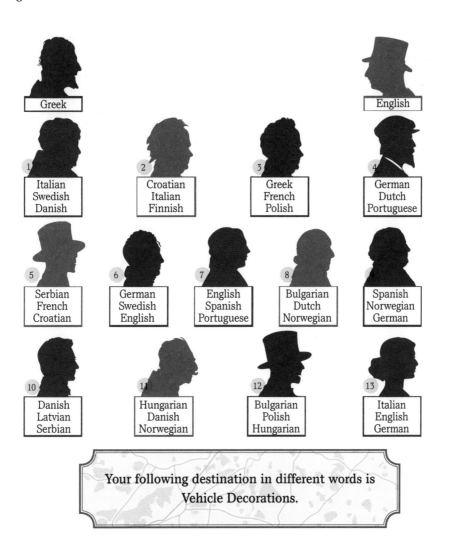

Greek

English

1
Italian
Swedish
Danish

2
Croatian
Italian
Finnish

3
Greek
French
Polish

4
German
Dutch
Portuguese

5
Serbian
French
Croatian

6
German
Swedish
English

7
English
Spanish
Portuguese

8
Bulgarian
Dutch
Norwegian

9
Spanish
Norwegian
German

10
Danish
Latvian
Serbian

11
Hungarian
Danish
Norwegian

12
Bulgarian
Polish
Hungarian

13
Italian
English
German

**Your following destination in different words is
Vehicle Decorations.**

Sherlock Holmes takes this case to heart and uses all the contacts he has at his disposal to try and gather as much information as possible. This is why the Greek consul receives these odd bits of paper. He quickly understands that they come from his famous acquaintance, Sherlock Holmes, and proceeds to transcribe them in the right order in the accompanying grid below.

What does Sherlock Holmes' message say? (If you know his address, it helps!)

On the map, go northwest to the
closest location.

6
Distance

"How far would you say you went in that carriage?" Sherlock Holmes asks the Greek interpreter. He was expecting some vague estimation, but Mr. Melas gave a very precise answer.

"How ever did you reach such a detailed estimate?" queries Holmes, somewhat incredulous.

"Well, as I entered the carriage," says Mr. Melas, "I saw that the top of the big wheel reached my elbow, which made it 1.5 yards high, which means that the circumference of the wheel was 4.7 yards. Later on during the journey, I noticed that this very wheel made an odd clicking sound every time it passed the mudguard at the top. Instinctively, I timed it, and there were 56 clicks a minute. Since it was quarter past seven when we left and my watch showed it was ten minutes to nine when at last we arrived . . . well, knowing that there are 1,760 yards in a mile, I just had to work it out."

Sherlock, amused and impressed by this punctilious man, checks if he can reach the same conclusion. And he does.

How far would you say the carriage traveled? (If this is the sort of question that reminds you too much of unpleasant school exercises for it to be fun, you may jump directly to the box below!)

For your next destination on the map, go
straight to number thirteen.

Multicycles

ycroft has an extraordinary faculty for figures, and as a result, he sometimes expresses himself in an unusual way. Talking about the stock of cycles at a nearby shop, he says, "All of Jenkins' cycles are monocycles, except for twenty-four wheels; all of Jenkins' cycles are bicycles, except for twenty-four wheels; and all of Jenkins' cycles are tricycles, except for twenty-four wheels."

Sherlock, having heard this sort of reasoning all his life, understands it right away. Watson finds it a little harder to understand.

How about you? How many monocycles, bicycles, and tricycles does Jenkins have in stock?

6

The number of monocycles minus one corresponds to the number of the next stop on the map.

Clocks Galore

After being released by his captors, and despite their threats, Mr. Melas goes straight to the police to tell his story. When he mentions that the room where he was detained had a large clock, the policeman suddenly becomes interested, hoping to have a lead on a gang of thieves who have been combing the area.

"What did this clock look like? Was it like one of these?" asks the officer.

Mr. Melas conscientiously looks over the pictures that are handed to him.

"Mmm . . . it wasn't that one in which you can't see the pendulum. The one I saw had a round pendulum, and you couldn't see the weights. It wasn't like that one, which doesn't give the same time as the others, and it didn't have little feet like this one. The name of the make wasn't written on it, and the clockface didn't have numerals. It wasn't like the tallest one here, nor indeed, like the shortest."

That only leaves one. Which one?

On a twenty-four-hour clock, it would be 1700 hours, but on a conventional clock, the hour hand would be on the figure that gives you your next stop.

Vehicle Tracks

When Sherlock and his companions arrive at The Myrtles, the cottage appears empty and many tracks in the muddy driveway suggest that the occupants have recently made a hurried escape. The tracks are easily identified by Holmes as being those of a light carriage, a heavy carriage, a handcart, a wheelbarrow, and a bicycle.

Each member of the group interprets these tracks, but one of the five is mistaken. In what order were these tracks made?

- Sherlock Holmes: Three tracks were made after the passage of the light carriage.
- Watson: The wheelbarrow passed after the handcart.
- Inspector Gregson: The light carriage came after the heavy carriage and the handcart.
- Mycroft: The bicycle passed before the handcart.
- Barry, the police assistant: The heavy carriage tracks were clearly the last.

For the next stop, move to knives and forks of yesteryear.

10
Carriage Ornaments

The poor Greek interpreter had found himself locked up in a carriage, with the windows obliterated with paper and a menacing keeper armed with a formidable-looking bludgeon. The drive had lasted for nearly two hours, and to ward off his fears, the interpreter had kept his mind busy on other subjects.

"What did you do?" asks Holmes, fascinated by this quiet, self-possessed man.

"I divided everything I could see by five!" he replies, unexpectedly.

The carriage was decorated with ornamental friezes and Mr. Melas found ways of dividing each one into five coherent sections. Can you?

The dictionary definition for your next stop is "the amount of space between two places or things."

Muddy Footprints

Mycroft and Sherlock like to compete with each other over the quantity of information they can glean from apparently banal footprints. Here, they see the footprints of a class of boys they are familiar with, and they have fun attributing each footprint to the boy it belongs to.

All the footprints come in pairs. The left footprint is accompanied by the beginning of the name and the right footprint with the end of the name. One footprint doesn't come with its corresponding pair.

"So," concludes Sherlock, "what's the name of the boy who only left one footprint?"

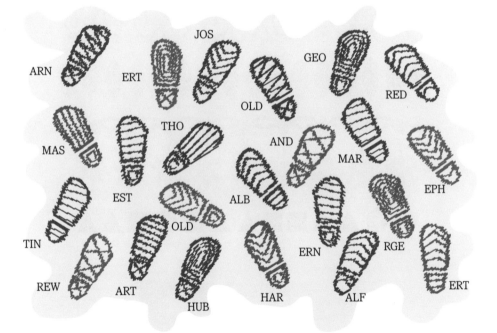

Go south on the map to reach the following
destination not far away.

Small Adds

Mycroft and the Greek interpreter took the matter further by placing an advertisement asking for information in most of the daily newspapers. They have received a few answers.

"The trouble with these small adds," comments Watson, "is that any fool can answer, and many do. Or people reply who are incapable of giving a straight answer. For example, look at this." The doctor hands Holmes a scruffy piece of paper.

"I imagine one is supposed to write a figure in the dotted space," says Holmes, "but that means that there are four . . . actually, five possible answers."

Find at least three possible answers.

> The person your are looking for lives in a house in Ransom Road. If you add up the ...... house numbers preceding the one of his house, you will reach a total of twenty-one.

The sum of the two numbers preceding ten will give you the number of your next destination on the map.

Sticking-Plaster Man

The Greek interpreter had to interrogate a poor man whose face was covered in sticking-plaster. The aim of his kidnappers was to make this man unrecognizable. But with the help of police artists, the interpreter must determine which drawing is most like the man with the sticking-plaster. Sherlock looks on, but his mind is elsewhere. In your opinion, which face below is most like number eight?

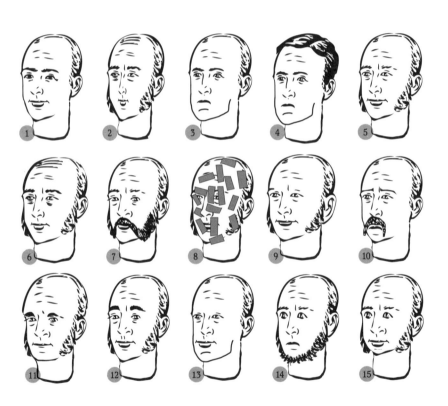

The number of the chosen face multiplied by four and plus two will give you the number of your next destination on the map.

Weapons

Before setting off to rescue the Greek interpreter the second time he is kidnapped, everyone is conscious that this could be a dangerous mission, and each member of the group brings a weapon. Well, almost everyone. Mycroft, for his part, brings his fountain pen, which could indeed be a frightful weapon in the press, but might not prove so effective against kidnappers. As for the others, a little light needs to be shed on the matter. The following conditions should make things clear:

- If Holmes brings a jackknife with him, then Barry, the inspector's assistant, has a revolver.
- If Watson brings a dagger, then Barry has a cudgel.
- If Inspector Gregson brings a dagger with him, then it is Watson who has a jackknife.
- If it isn't Holmes who brings a jackknife, then Watson brings a dagger.

Who brings which weapon?

There are three, and you can pass over or under them, but first, you must go there on the map.

Mycroft

Sherlock Holmes describes the nonchalant character of his brother to his friend, and notably says of him:

trouble to

Mycroft

be considered

rather

prove

wrong than

would

himself right

take the

Place the word fragments in the right order to form Sherlock's description of his brother.

Count the number of letters in the penultimate word in the description of Mycroft. That is the number of your next destination on the map.

Book Binding

"Did you notice that book?" Holmes asks Watson on their way home, after the intervention at The Myrtles cottage.

"No, what book are you talking about?" asks Watson.

"You know, the books that were extremely untidy on the shelf at the top of the stairs. And one was bound all wrong!"

Watson looks at his friend in astonishment. "Do you mean to say that as we were rushing up those stairs to save poor Mr. Melas, you had time to check out the books?"

"Well, it was pretty outstanding, you have to admit!" confirms Holmes.

Which book below is Holmes talking about?

The name of the following stop suggests
a conclusion or an afterthought.

Flower Cottages

An answer to the advertisement in the newspaper arrives and Sherlock Holmes is convinced that it is genuine. It reveals that the house where the man with sticking-plaster on his face is being held captive is at Beckenham and is called The Myrtles.

Country houses are often named after flowers, and below are some examples.Each group of letters can be rearranged to form the name of a flower, and then the first letter of each one of these flowers can also be rearranged to form yet another flower. What is this final flower that is also the name of a nearby cottage?

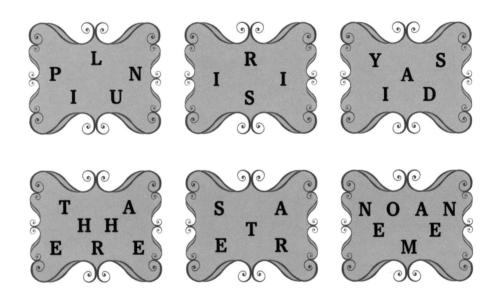

For your next stop on the map, go to the distant Keyword.

Brother

Shortly after telling Watson that he has a brother, Sherlock invites his friend to meet him at the Diogenes Club. Shortly after, Sherlock and Watson arrive at the very select club, where, in the muted atmosphere, Watson has his first glimpse of Mycroft Holmes. However, there are six gentlemen present, each one in his bubble of indifference to the others.

"Which one is your brother?" whispers Watson.

"He's the one with Thaddeus to his right and Obediah to his left," replies Sherlock in a low voice.

"And where are they?" queries Watson in a hushed tone.

"There are two people between Obediah and Batholomew. Enoch isn't at Reuben's right, but farther to the right than Mycroft and Batholomew."

"Ah," sighs Watson, having at last spotted the elusive brother.

Can you locate Mycroft?

To find your next stop on the map,
go southwest for a short distance.

Clapham Junction

The Greek interpreter was abandoned by his kidnappers in the middle of nowhere, but after walking for a while, he saw a sign announcing CLAPHAM JUNCTION. A bush partially hid the P, so only the syllables CLA and HAM were visible.

"So, on my return journey," explains Mr. Melas to Sherlock Holmes, "I searched for words with those two syllables."

Three letters of each word below can be covered with either CLA or HAM to make other words. Find these words.

CLA	HAM
MONSTER	HORRIFY
DENTURE	BULLETS
FARMERS	CALIBER
GROWING	STINGER
STUBBLE	ELIXIRS

CLAPHAM JUNCTION

The name of the next stop can make you think of multiple and sonorous ticktocks.

The Three-Bridge Route

The cottage where the Greek interpreter is probably being held captive is in a remote spot, and Sherlock and his companions ask a local policeman how to get there.

"It's not that far," he replies, "but there have been floods, and the only safe way is the route which passes by no more than three bridges—above or below."

Find the three-bridge route!

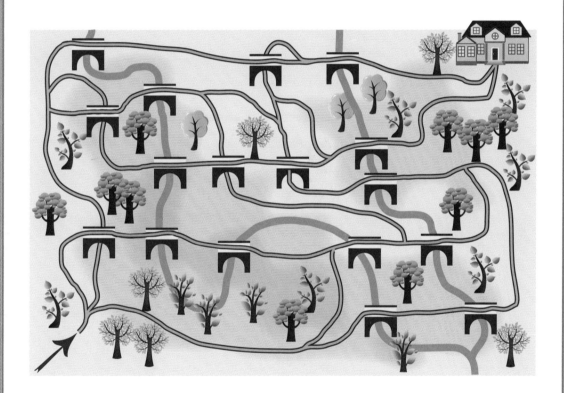

> Three times the number of bridges taken
> is the number of the next destination
> on the map.

Card Finder

A t the Diogenes Club, Mycroft is profoundly absorbed, contemplating some playing cards. He is engrossed in a very Holmesian activity. He challenges himself to find a question that will apply to all these cards and will have a single solution.

In this instance, he invents the following question: Which card has the same suit as three others and comes from the same deck of cards as three others, no more, no less? There are four decks of cards (red, green, blue, and gray) that can be distinguished by the back of the card just under each card.

Which one is Mycroft's card?

The main character of this scene is also the name of
the next destination on the map.

Text on a Slate

The Greek interpreter explains to Sherlock Holmes what he has been through and how he was forced to interrogate a poor defenseless man. The people who captured this man were suspicious, and they only allowed their prisoner to give answers by writing them on a slate. However, the poor man soon realized that no one other than the interpreter could fully understand what he wrote in Greek. He saw in this an opportunity to communicate secret information.

Below is an English equivalent of one of the prisoner's answers. It contains a hidden message. Can you decipher this hidden message within the message?

> No aount of miser ca mke e agre to ther devilih lans. Whtever they make me sffer, I shal resist, nowing pefectly well tht hey are ruthless indivduals an that thy may lay me.

On the same principle, your next stop is N°:

.obody .s .egotiating, not .ven .he .xtremely .nvious .oblemen.

Watson's Version

"At this stage, Watson," Sherlock Holmes asks his friend, "how would you sum up the situation?"

Watson thinks as he talks, but his reply comes out in a scrambled way. Put the following phrases in order to make a coherent narrative.

and this man, Harold, persuades her to flee

get an interpreter and choose Mr. Melas.

Greece and imprudently puts himself into the

make him sign some papers to make over

order to negotiate with him they have to

power of the young man and his associate.

Sophy, a Greek girl, comes on a visit to England,

the girl's fortune. This he refuses to do. In

They use violence towards him in order to

with him. Then her brother comes over from

Put this sentence in the right order and go there on the map: The next of your multiplied is destination two number by six.

Some months later, Sherlock Holmes is in his study reflecting on the tragic affair of the Greek interpreter when he comes across a newspaper article precisely on this case. Two Englishmen had been found stabbed to death in Hungary. The Greek lady who accompanied them explained to the police that during a quarrel, they had inflicted these wounds upon each other.

Sherlock's view on the matter can be found below. To read it, you must find the first letter, then skip regularly over three letters. It's up to you to decide whether to read clockwise or counterclockwise.

This brings this chapter to a conclusion and the occasion for you to find the fifth hidden word in the Sherlock Challenge.

CHAPTER 6
The Bruce-Partington Plans

"The Adventure of the Bruce-Partington Plans" can be seen as a precursor to modern spy stories, with its stolen military plans, international agents, murder, and treachery, but it is also a wonderfully atmospheric adventure in a smog-ridden London. This smog also plays an important part in the story, hiding what normally can be seen and making everything slightly mysterious.

Sherlock Holmes is at his best here, questioning the obvious and discovering that the unlikely is sometimes the only possible explanation. This story also brings back that wonderful character, the portly, phlegmatic Mycroft Holmes. We discover that his role in government is considerably more important than had been suggested previously, and in this story, he is in a spot of trouble and is very lucky to have the help of his bright brother, for the plans for a top-secret submarine have been stolen and must be snatched out of the hands of foreign spies.

You will need to sharpen your wits and keep to Sherlock Holmes' high standards to find all the solutions to the following puzzles.

As explained in the introduction, use the map on pages 150–151 as a travel map. It will be essential to guide you through the strange places and events of this story to the final solving of the case.

Start with the first puzzle on page 152. Once you have solved it, follow the clue in the box at the bottom of the page to find your next destination on the map. This location comes with a number that gives you the number of the next puzzle you need to solve. Continue in this way, going back and forth, from puzzle to map, until you reach the last puzzle of the adventure. Have fun on your journey!

The Bruce-Partington Plans

START

LONDON

13. Burglar's Kit

23. Housebreaking

A

1. Foggy Times

14. Ars Antiqua

21. Timetable

LAMBETH

10. Appreciation

20. Old Axiom

24. Royal Gratitude

CAMBERWELL

18. Police Report

BECKHAM

9. Messenger Pigeons

BRIXTON

12. Double Cypher

17. Weighty Poison

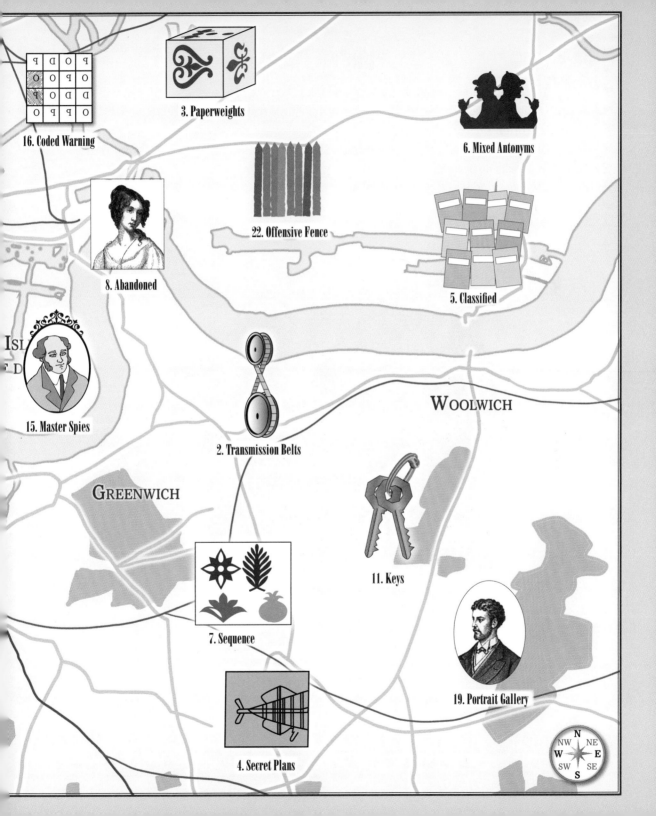

16. Coded Warning

3. Paperweights

6. Mixed Antonyms

22. Offensive Fence

8. Abandoned

5. Classified

ISL
E D

15. Master Spies

WOOLWICH

2. Transmission Belts

GREENWICH

11. Keys

7. Sequence

19. Portrait Gallery

4. Secret Plans

N
NW NE
W E
SW SE
S

1
Foggy Times

A dense fog has settled on London and made travel and almost any other activity impossible. Poor Sherlock Holmes is incredibly restless, craving action in this grayish cotton-wool atmosphere.

During a short walk, the fog is so dense that he has difficulty reading the time on the various clocks he passes.

In what order did he come upon these clocks?

(A)　　　(B)　(C)　　(D)　　(E)　　　(F)

From nineteenth-century, foggy London,
jump to the art of medieval Europe on the map.

2

Transmission Belts

As Sherlock Holmes is to discover, among the many secret features of the Bruce-Partington submarine is a complex mechanism of transmission belts. This is explained in detail, of course, in the stolen documents.

Below is a small and simple extract from these plans. If the big wheel turns in the direction as shown, does the belt below it move upward or downward?

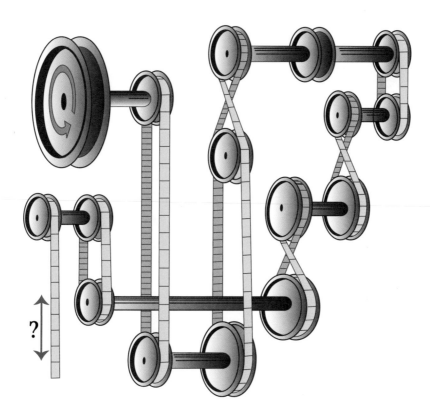

On the map, go in the same direction
as the belt in question until you reach
your next destination.

Paperweights

While Sherlock Holmes searches for evidence in room after room at Caulfield Gardens, he comes across some little, decorated cubes that are probably used as paperweights.

"How strange to have so many identical objects," comments Watson.

"No, they're not all identical. One is different from the others," corrects Holmes.

Find the cube below that is different from all the others.

For your next destination on the map,
look for a title meaning "discourteous palisade."

4

Secret Plans

"Why take the plans themselves and risk being caught, rather than just copying them?" asks Watson.

"Because the plans are so complex," replies a senior member of the Admiralty, "that it is difficult to copy them without making mistakes. Take this one, for instance. It was copied by a very able draftsman, but he made ten mistakes, which would have fatal consequences."

Find the ten mistakes.

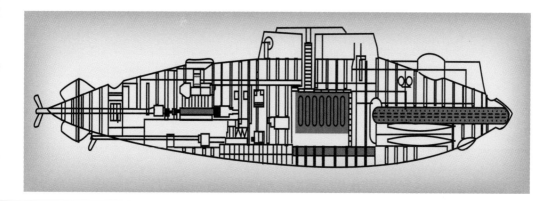

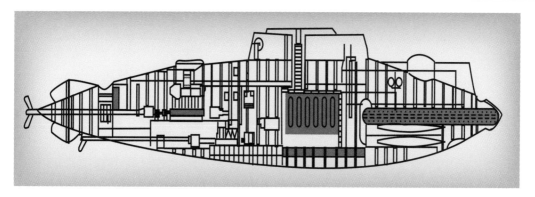

On the map, go to
a gallery of portraits.

Classified

Sherlock Holmes looks over the folders of the stolen documents. "So, which ones are missing?" he asks the clerk.

"Er, hem," mumbles the senior clerk. "I'm, er, not allowed to say . . . but, er, hem, I could say that, er, disregarding the letters, the total of the numbers of the three stolen documents adds up to ninety-five."

"I see," says Sherlock.

Which documents were stolen?

CLASSIFIED
AW 45

CLASSIFIED
AX 13

CLASSIFIED
AY 44

CLASSIFIED
BY 24

CLASSIFIED
CF 54

CLASSIFIED
DE 30

CLASSIFIED
GL 21

CLASSIFIED
HX 08

CLASSIFIED
HY 47

CLASSIFIED
HZ 65

Add together the figures of the highest number above, and you'll come up with a two-digit number. Now, add together these two digits for your next destination on the map.

Mixed Antonyms

On discovering the identity of the traitor, Sherlock Holmes is so surprised that he cries out, "You can write me down an ass this time, Watson." This most unusual moment of self-criticism comes from the fact that in this adventure, contradictory and conflicting forces are profoundly intertwined.

In this fashion, you will find contradictory words mixed together to become almost incomprehensible. In each set of letters below, two antonyms are mixed together, but the order of the letters of each word remains unchanged.

Find the antonyms.

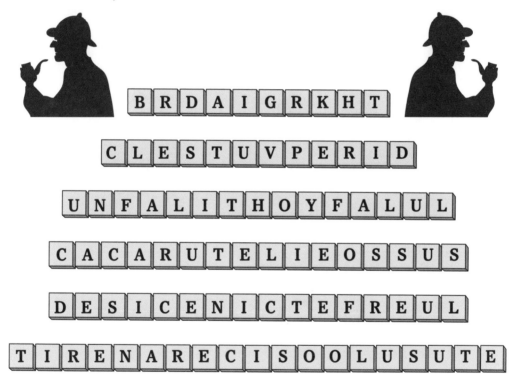

B R D A I G R K H T

C L E S T U V P E R I D

U N F A L I T H O Y F A L U L

C A C A R U T E L I E O S S U S

D E S I C E N I C T E F R E U L

T I R E N A R E C I S O O L U S U T E

> Mixing together the two words of the title of your next stop in the same way as the words above gives MESPIGSENEONGERS.

Sequence

W hen Sherlock Holmes goes to the Woolwich Arsenal office, he can't help noticing that some of their "secret" methods are known to every schoolboy in the country. To mark a sequence, for instance, they use the simple system of symbols, in pairs.

For example, with the sets below, start with box A and move to another box that contains at least two identical symbols. Then, from that box, move on to another one that also shares two identical symbols. Continue in this way, finding a route that passes by the nine boxes. Which is the last box of the sequence?

 Take the letter of the final set found above, convert it to a number (A=1, B=2, etc.), and then multiply that number by 4. That's your next stop on the map.

✣ 8 ✣
Abandoned

"We were walking, and suddenly, without a word, Arthur . . . I mean Mr. Cadogan West, my fiancé, darted away into the fog. I waited, but he never returned."

Had Miss Violet Westbury not been so much in love, she could, very justifiably, have considered that she had been rudely abandoned.

Words with a meaning close to "abandoned" have been cut in half and strewn about the page below. Another word with a completely different meaning has also been cut in half and mixed in with the rest. Can you find the words, along with the odd one out?

DESE   AKEN   CTED   WAY   JIL

OSTRA

DISCA   ECTED   DITC   RTED

NDED

FORGO   TED   IFIED   NGED

HED

DROP   NEGL

IATED

ESTRA   REPUD   REJE

CLASS

STRA   FORS

CASTA   PED

RDED

TTEN   CIZED

The odd word out gives you the title of your next stop on the map.

Messenger Pigeons

Holmes wants to know where the most active spying activity is taking place in order to direct his investigation. So, Mycroft shows him a secret-service report on the busiest messenger-pigeon routes in Europe. This is a means of communication mainly used by the various secret services and private spies.

"I see where we should be concentrating our attention," comments Holmes.

Pigeon flights connect flags with identical numbers. Where is the busiest intersection?

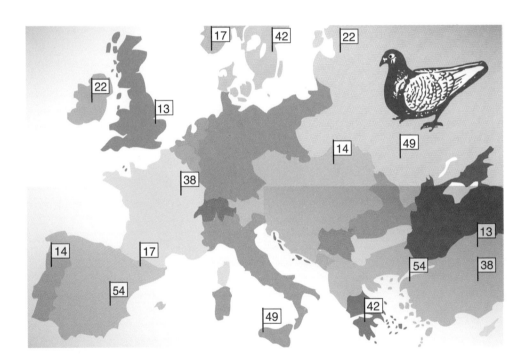

The number on the flag farthest north on the map above gives you the number of your next stop on the travel map.

Appreciation

When Sherlock Holmes starts investigating the Case of the Bruce-Partington Plans, a police officer explains that they are not playing according to the same rules. Sherlock occasionally chooses to disregard the law, whereas the police must keep to strict legality.

Sherlock Holmes and a police officer both make a remark on Holmes' position in respect to the law, but their remarks are mixed up!

Separate the two sentences below without changing the order of the words.

It is it fortunate is a mercy for that this you are on community the side that I of the force am not and not against a criminal it

On the map, move northeast until you come to a stop. That is your next destination.

At the time of Sherlock Holmes' investigation, two people possess the three keys to reach the safe. A few years earlier, there were five keys and eight people had copies of some of the keys but not others. To reach the precious documents, however, each key had to be used with a duplicate. This made for some complications, hence the change in organization.

In order to have a duplicate of each key, which of the five people below would you ask?

The title of your next stop on the map could be reworded as thus: people, superior to their peers, who obtain secret information.

Sherlock Holmes has discovered that the spies he is tracking communicate by placing advertisements in the newspaper. He decides to use this discovery to trick one of them into running into a trap he has set up in advance.

He puzzles out the code and discovers that the first advertisement contains the message "Come at four." A little later, he has the second message inserted into the newspaper. Can you discover the hidden message it contains?

First message sent by the spies:

> TRANSACTIONS
>
> The administrative acceptance procedure for Smiths Ltd. is too imminent to foresee Isaacs and Co's reactions beforehand. The company has omitted from the invoice most unaffordable goods such as the vacuum override.

Trap message sent by Sherlock Holmes:

> LEISURE
>
> Write to Jimmy Green to reserve a week's vacation in attractive skiing resort. For customers planning to stay longer, we can offer a full equipment at our special ski bazaar, at little more than cost price.

A tiepin indicates the location of your
next and last stop on the map.

Burglar's Kit

Sherlock asks Watson to meet him with all the tools necessary to break in to a house. This not being a habit of Watson's, he has to go to a nearby shop to buy the necessary equipment.

The salesman, a gruff and grumpy fellow, tells him that the lots below are being sold at £15, £16, £18, £26, £28, and £36. And if he wants to buy some tools and not others, then he can jolly well work out the price of each!

The tools, luckily, do not vary in price from one lot to another, but the salesman didn't give the prices in the order the lots are presented.

Watson really needs a lamp. What's the price of that? All tools cost a round number of pounds.

 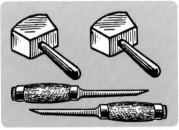 

The price of a revolver and a chisel
gives you in pounds the number of
your next stop on the map.

The fog and professional inactivity make Sherlock Holmes restless, but he keeps busy with his hobby: the music of the Middle Ages. He adds the final touches to his monograph on the Polyphonic Motets of Lassus, which will be printed a few months later to much acclaim by experts on the subject.

In keeping with this passion, you will find in the grids below many words related to medieval music. Some words appear in one grid, some in the other, and one in both grids. Can you spot them? They are written in all directions, including diagonally.

ArsAntiqua
ArsNova
baroque
bass
canon
canticles
choir
dulcimer
earthly
Gregorian
instrumental
Josquin
Lassus
lute
Machaut
madrigal
modes
motet
octave
organum
Palestrina
pipes
plainchant
polyphonic
queen
recorder
rondeau
sacred
secular
song
troubadours
trouvere
vocal
Victoria

P	I	P	E	S	B	X	X
X	M	A	C	H	A	U	T
L	Y	L	H	T	R	A	E
U	A	E	D	N	O	R	T
G	R	S	X	E	Q	E	O
R	S	T	S	E	U	D	M
E	A	R	X	U	E	R	X
G	N	I	U	Q	S	O	J
O	T	N	O	N	A	C	S
R	I	A	M	O	D	E	S
I	Q	C	H	O	I	R	A
A	U	L	A	C	O	V	B
N	A	D	E	R	C	A	S
M	A	D	R	I	G	A	L

A	R	S	N	O	V	A	I
S	X	R	C	V	P	X	N
O	T	U	A	I	O	T	S
N	R	O	N	C	L	N	T
G	O	D	T	T	Y	A	R
X	U	A	I	O	P	H	U
R	V	B	C	R	H	C	M
E	E	U	L	I	O	N	E
M	R	O	E	A	N	I	N
I	E	R	S	X	I	A	T
C	E	T	U	L	C	L	A
L	A	S	S	U	S	P	L
U	M	U	N	A	G	R	O
D	S	E	C	U	L	A	R

4

On the map, go to the stop with the same number as the total number of Xs in the grids above (the Xs aren't part of any words).

15
Master Spies

"So, who are the master spies these days?" Holmes asks Mycroft.

"Well, there are three main ones and two upstarts who need watching. They are Adolph Meyer, Louis La Rothière, Hugo Oberstein, Sergio Malavista, and Piotr Volovitch. Look, we have portraits of them, in case you should meet them—"

"Aha," interjects Sherlock. "And who is who?"

Mycroft being Mycroft, he is incapable of giving a straight answer and says, rather laboriously, "As you see them here, Adolph Meyer is farther to the left than Louis La Rothière. There is one person between Hugo Oberstein and Sergio Malavista and two between Sergio Malavista and Piotr Volovitch. And this Piotr fellow is next to the Frenchy, Louis La Rothière. There, now you know everything."

Can you pair each portrait with the correct spy?

On the map, go northeast
to the nearest destination.

Coded Warning

When searching through the flat in Caulfield Gardens, Sherlock flips through numerous books; opens boxes; reads notes, memos, and letters; and generally sifts through all the available evidence.

However, there is one envelope that he leaves unopened. When Watson asks him why, he replies, "There's this little grid on it, and I believe it's a warning for the person receiving it. I've seen this system used elsewhere. You see the square colored in green? Well, you have to color in three more squares in green so that they are all in different rows, columns, and diagonals. You then proceed the same way with the square colored in red. A first word can then be read on the green squares, a second on the red, and a third on the uncolored squares.

What message can one read?

P	O	D	O
O	I	S	P
E	O	N	N
E	T	N	D

> The next stop concerns a weighty object used to keep lighter objects from flying about all over the place.

Weighty Poison

As if solving one of the most complex cases wasn't enough to keep his mind busy, Holmes occupies his downtime with studying the comparative weights of poisonous substances.

Once he has established that all bottles of the same color have the same weight, he manages to classify these poisons from the lightest to the heaviest.

With the help of the scales below, discover for yourself the comparative weights of these toxic substances.

The next destination on the map
is twice a code.

Police Report

Sherlock Holmes is invited by the police department to a meeting in which they are discussing the case of Cadogan West. The detective remains silent, taking in information and sharpening his own ideas on the case.

The present working hypothesis is that the body of Cadogan West was thrown out of a moving Underground train carriage onto the tracks.

Here are some of the police reports on this case:

- Only someone who had access to the tracks could have moved the body.

- The body had lost a lot of blood.
- The only employees who have access to the tracks are also those who have special keys which open carriage doors.
- No evidence of violence was found in any carriage.
- The body was too heavy for a senior employee to displace it.
- No blood was found on the tracks near the body.
- Only senior Underground employees have access to the tracks.

And here are a few conclusions. Which ones are logically coherent with the preceding statements?

A • It must be an Underground employee who threw Cadogan West out of a carriage.

B • Since no blood was found near the body, it must have been moved.

C • The victim must have been killed in the carriage.

D • A senior employee is clearly responsible for the murder.

E • The evidence shows that the working hypothesis is wrong somewhere.

> The name of your next stop on the map signifies "tools for housebreakers."

Portrait Gallery

"Do you have a list of all the people who are authorized to see these papers?" Sherlock asks Sir John Walter, the official guardian of the secret documents at the Admiralty.

"We have better than that!" boasts Sir John. "We have the names and the portraits of the members of the three authorized teams. Look, here they are. But they are all absolutely irreproachable, I assure you."

The names are given alphabetically and not in the order of the pictures. Match the names with their portraits.

P. J. Harmond
O. D. Johnsteen
F. W. Karsley
S. A. Maximus

B. B. Debs
P. J. Harmond
S. A. Maximus
R. H. Raphaels

C. U. Creight
P. J. Harmond
F. W. Karsley
R. H. Raphaels

> Count the number of letters in the names of the two women above (excluding initials). This is the number of your next destination.

When Sherlock suggests that Cadogan West was *on* the roof of the carriage, rather than *in* it, Watson objects that it seems most improbable, to which Sherlock replies, "We must fall back upon the old axiom that . . ."

Complete Sherlock's reply by moving from one bubble to the next, as long as they are connected with a dotted line.

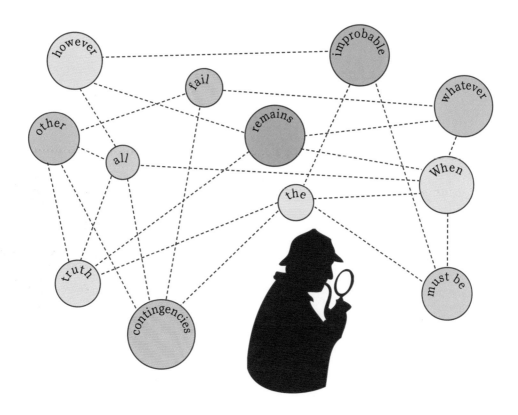

> The direction taken between the last two words is
> the same as the one you must take on the map to
> reach your next stop.

Timetable

The body of Cadogan West, an employee closely related to the stolen top-secret plans, has been found on the railroad tracks!

"For the sake of argument, let us suppose that Cadogan West entered the Underground at Westminster at quarter to eight. Could he reach Algate before ten," asks Watson, "taking into account the odd timetable at the moment, with all these works and stations temporarily closed?"

"If he had a thorough knowledge of the timetable then, yes, it would be possible," confirms Holmes.

Find on the timetable below the journey from Westminster at quarter to eight to Algate before ten.

Westbound		Station	Eastbound		
• 8.26		South Kensington	• 7.54		• 8.29
		Sloane Square		• 8.19	• 8.39
• 8.08		Victoria	• 8.12	• 8.27	• 8.47
	• 10.11	St James Park		• 8.38	• 8.54
• 7.53		Westminster	• 8.27		• 9.02
	• 9.53	Charing Cross	• 8.47		
• 7.52	• 9.42	Temple			• 9.23
		Blackfriars		• 9.21	
• 7.21	• 9.31	Mansion House			• 9.34
	• 9.27	Cannon street	• 9.29	• 9.25	
• 7.11		Monument		• 9.46	• 9.44
	• 9.16	Mark Lane		• 9.56	• 9.50
• 7.00	• 9.11	Algate			• 9.57

3 The number of trains needed to reach the destination with the timetable above is the number of the next stop on the map.

Offensive Fence

The angry writing on the fence is no longer readable. The boards have been taken down and then put up again in a different order—possibly by the police, who did not like what it said.

Sherlock Holmes manages to put the boards in the right order in his head, and he is not displeased by what he reads. What do you make of it? The first and last boards have not been moved.

Above, Sherlock Holmes is pointing
in the direction you must take on the map
to reach your next stop.

Housebreaking

Occasionally, Sherlock Holmes deliberately breaks the law. When he decides to force his way into the abandoned house of the master spy, he does so without a warrant or any form of permission from the police. Indeed, when Watson sets off with the housebreaking equipment, he hopes that he won't be stopped by a policeman, for he would be at pains to justify himself.

Three words that could qualify Sherlock and Watson's activities are given below. To find them, imagine that every blue circle is placed on top of one of the green circles, turning it around, if necessary, so that the letters form an eight-letter word. Find which circles fit together and what words they spell.

The next stop on the map is a warning, but as always with Holmes, not quite straightforward.

Royal Gratitude

For his eminent role in saving secret plans from enemy hands, Sherlock Holmes is received at Buckingham Palace. He returns with a precious emerald tiepin, and he is as discreet about this gift as he is about the whole adventure.

To find which one is his tiepin, all you need to know is that it is different from all the others.

With this puzzle, dear reader, you have reached the last of the adventures in this book. Now you can find the final hidden word in the Sherlock Challenge and decipher the quotation!

The Sherlock Challenge

Grids to Fill In

With your magnifying-glass number, go to the grid of the chapter, find the word with that number and write it out in the first line of the grid. Write the following words, line after line, in the order the numbers are given.

Chapter 1. The Mazarin Stone

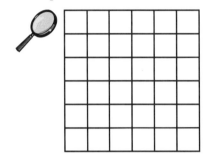

1. CACTUS	5. PRAISE
2. CHANCE	6. RABBIT
3. EASILY	7. STRING
4. HEALTH	8. TEAPOT

Chapter 2. Wisteria Lodge

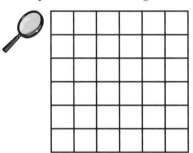

1. BOUNCE	5. MORSEL
2. DEBATE	6. RATTLE
3. EAGLES	7. SANITY
4. ELDERS	8. SEARCH

Chapter 3. The Second Stain

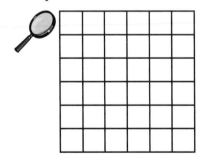

1. ACTIVE	5. LIKELY
2. ADMIRE	6. RAGGED
3. DEPUTY	7. SAILOR
4. FAMILY	8. STAPLE

Chapter 4. The Reigate Puzzle

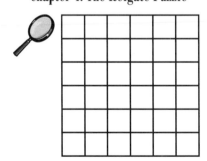

1. BITTER	5. MEDIUM
2. COHORT	6. RIDDLE
3. DIALOG	7. SELDOM
4. GERBIL	8. WEALTH

Chapter 5. The Greek Interpreter

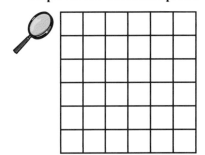

1. ENERGY
2. GEYSER
3. IRONIC
4. LENGTH
5. PACKET
6. PENCIL
7. RANGER
8. VIKING

Chapter 6. The Bruce-Partington Plans

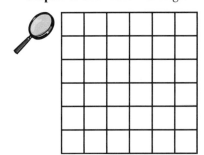

1. CHAIRS
2. LEADER
3. NINETY
4. OCCUPY
5. PRINCE
6. SUBTLE
7. TAILOR
8. TOFFEE

Hidden Words

Once a grid is completed, look for the hidden six-letter word it contains. It can be written in all directions, up, down, or diagonally, then write it out in the corresponding space just below.

Chapter 1

1 2 3 4 5 6

Chapter 2

7 8 9 10 11 12

Chapter 3

13 14 15 16 17 18

Chapter 4

19 20 21 22 23 24

Chapter 5

25 26 27 28 29 30

Chapter 6

31 32 33 34 35 36

Quote Finder

Once the six words have been found, transcribe the letters into the quote finder below, placing the letters according to their number. You will complete a Sherlock Holmes quotation beginning with "It has long been an axiom of mine that . . . "

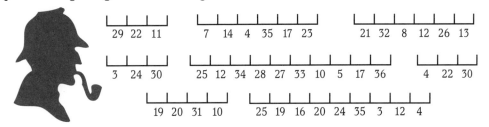

29 22 11

7 14 4 35 17 23

21 32 8 12 26 13

3 24 30

25 12 34 28 27 33 10 5 17 36

4 22 30

19 20 31 10

25 19 16 20 24 35 3 12 4

Answers to The Mazarin Stone

1. Silhouette 4. Differences: 1. Pipe arm shorter 2. Top of armchair 3. Position of lower leg 5. Inclination of the head 6. Pipe arm more vertical 7. Foot turned upward. *Go to #6 on the map.*

2. 10 pairs of handcuffs. All the handcuffs are connected except for two pairs.
Go to #24 on the map.

3. This segment should have 3 white and 3 black pips. Each segment has a different number of black and white pips, ranging from 0 to 6, but with one number missing: 3. Turning the parasol in a clockwise direction, the number of white pips increases by one, in every other segment. The same rule applies to the black pips, but by turning the parasol in a counterclockwise direction.
Go to #8 on the map.

4. SALOON which can only be transformed into SALMON (or the rare SALOOP), neither of which are tools. The other transformations: HAMPER - HAMMER, TRENCH -WRENCH, BUTTER - CUTTER, MULLET - MALLET, SWEARS - SHEARS, SCALPED - SCALPEL, CHAMP - CLAMP, SHADE - SPADE, BRASH - BRUSH. *Go to #13 on the map.*

5. Top triangle: 1. Bottom triangle: 10. Each large triangle plus the one just above it add up to 15. The small triangles that are pointing down on the top row are equal to the difference of the two triangles (pointing up) on either side of the triangles pointing down.
Go to #2 on the map.

6. Watson looked round at the scientific charts, the bench of chemicals, the violin-case, the coal-scuttle.
Go to #23 on the map.

W	A	T	S	O	N		L	O	O	K	E	D		R	O	U	N	D		A	T		T	H
E		S	C	I	E	N	T	I	F	I	C		C	H	A	R	T	S		T	H	E		B
E	N	C	H		O	F		C	H	E	M	I	C	A	L	S		T	H	E		V	I	O
L	I	N	-	C	A	S	E		T	H	E		C	O	A	L	-	S	C	U	T	T	L	E

7. Sherlock has been on the heels of character 4.
It is not 1, who is a man, but doesn't have a hat.
It is not 2, who is a woman, but she isn't holding anything.
It is not 6, who has a hat, but no flower.
It is not 3, who is holding a hat, but has a cane.
It is not 5, who has a necklace, but whose shoes are hidden.
This leaves 4. *Go to #17 on the map.*

8. Three of spades. The red card has the same value as the two black cards added together. Each hand has a red card, a clubs, and a spades. *Go to #15 on the map.*

9. Connector 2 should be placed. *Go to #11 on the map.*

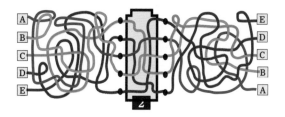

10. 54 years. The prison sentence is proportional to the value of the theft, so for every £5 stolen, the culprit is condemned to a day in prison.
£1,000=200 days, or 28 weeks and 4 days.
£1,830=366 days, or 1 year and 1 day.
£23,000=4,600 days, or 12 years (+4 days for leap years), 30 weeks, and 6 days.
£100,000=20,000 days, or 54 years (+13 days for leap years), 39 weeks, and 4 days.
Go to #22 on the map.

11. Watson is followed to the British Museum, but in fact, it was NOT his destination. Watson had spotted the man following him, so he took him to the British Museum, where he easily tricked him and got away to his real destination: Scotland Yard. *Go to #7 on the map.*

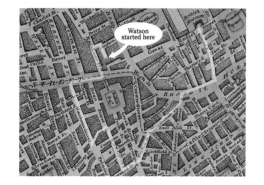

12. One can delete YOUR LORDSHIP, MY LADY BARONESS, HIS GRACIOUS HIGHNESS. *Go to #3 on the map.*

13. The Mazarin Stone, £90,000; El Distio, £4,500; Bleintheim, £3,700; Poseidon, £1,800. *Go to #9 on the map.*

14. Sylvius - Sam, Petrovitch - Hank, Darius - Ned, Greystone - Bert, Jackwort - Eddy, Harvey - Ian, Angelini - Gus. The first letters of the required henchmen form the word BEING. *Go to #21 on the map.*

15. PRISON.

Wealth	Poverty
Dated	Recent
Outside	Inside
Failure	Success
Mandatory	Optional
Clad	Naked

Go to #10 on the map.

16. PRECIOUS. *Go to #5 on the map.*

17. Left: Lord Cantlemere, who is convinced Holmes will fail.
Middle: The prime minister, who is convinced Holmes will succeed.
Right: The home secretary, who is not sure of Holmes' success.
The gentleman on the right cannot be talking to the prime minister since he mentions him. He cannot be talking to the home secretary, because the person he is addressing is convinced that Holmes will fail, while the home secretary isn't sure. So, he can only be talking to Lord Cantlemere (and therefore, Lord Cantlemere is sure Holmes will fail.) The man on the left is neither the prime minister nor the Lord, so he must be the home secretary. The gentleman on the left isn't addressing the home secretary (who has doubts about Holmes and is on the right), so he is talking to the person in the middle, and someone who thinks Holmes will succeed. This cannot be Lord Cantlemere, who thinks he will fail, nor the home secretary, who has doubts, so it can only be the prime minister, and he is in the middle, which leaves Lord Cantlemere on the left. *Go to #20 on the map.*

18. East Siders, 7; Chapel Gang, 3; The Greats, 9; Savvys, 2; Bossy Gees, 5; Fisty Kids, 8; Crazy Karters, 4; Tinny Uglies, 10; Kellyonians, 6. *Go to #19 on the map.*

19. COME BACK WITH THE POLICE. The key to the code is the number of the address. 136 for the first message means that the first letter is replaced with a 1-letter shift in the alphabet, the second letter a 3-letter shift, and the third letter a 6-letter shift. Thus, Z+1=A, A+3=D, X+6=D. This is repeated throughout the message. The second message is preceded with the number 35, so the first letter has a 3-letter shift and the second a 5-letter shift, and this is repeated to the end. Z+3=C, J+5=O, J+3=M, Z+5=E, etc. Map clue: TERMS OF ADDRESS. *Go to #12 on the map.*

20. HENCHMEN. The other anagrams: BEARD, WHISKERS, SIDEBURNS, STUBBLE, GOATEE.
Go to #14 on the map.

21. 9 is unique. The matching pairs:
1 - 15, 2 - 6, 3 - 13, 4 - 12, 5 - 7, 8 - 10, 11 - 14.
Go to #18 on the map.

22. ACTION. *Go to #16 on the map.*

23. 1. East Star 2. Yellow Empress 3. Karloff 4. Mazarin Stone.
The East Star is either 1 or 2, so it can't be 3, and that means that 2 is the Yellow Empress. Therefore, the East Star is not 2, which means that 1 is the East Star and that 4 is not the Karloff. Since the Karloff isn't 4, then it must be 3, which leaves 4 for the Mazarin Stone. *Go to #4 on the map.*

24. The word on the cubes: SUCCESS.
The grid on the right represents one of the cubes as if it were folded out. By observing the position of the letters on one face in respect to the ones on adjacent faces, one can establish the layout of the cubes.

Answers to Wisteria Lodge

1. PLEASE ARRANGE YOUR THOUGHTS COMMA AND LET ME KNOW WHAT EVENTS HAVE SENT YOU HERE STOP.
BL in front of AND spells BLAND. *Go to #10 on the map.*

2. On Mondays, four of the same kind and at least one blue: 4.
On Tuesdays, at least one blue and three yellow: 4 or 1, but 4 is Mondays, so 1.
On Wednesdays, four of the same kind and three or more different types: 3.
On Thursdays, three yellow: 5.
On Fridays, two white: 2.
Go to #16 on the map.

3. Mr. Henderson, 55; Miss Burnet, 44; Mr. Lucas, 35; Eliza, 11; Gladys, 9.
Miss Burnet (B) 2 years ago was 6 times as old as Gladys (G): $B-2=6(G-2)$, or $B=6(G-2)+2$.
Miss Burnet is 4 times the age of Eliza, who is 2 years older than Gladys: $B=4(G+2)$. This gives us $6(G-2)+2=4(G+2)$, from which we find that $G=9$. So, Gladys is 9, Eliza 11, and Miss Burnet 44. Mr. Lucas is B-G (44-9), and Mr Henderson is L+E+G (35+11+9).
Go to #23 on the map.

4. BY THE TIME YOU DECIPHER THIS, HOLMES, I WILL BE FAR AWAY ENJOYING MY ILL-GOTTEN FORTUNE. The text is camouflaged, simply by inverting the order of every successive pair of letters. YB=BY, YB HTT E=BY THE T. The spaces between words of the original text remain unchanged. AMSNOIN: MANSION. *Go to #11 on the map.*

5. HYENA, SHARK, EAGLE. With vowels, the word spells POLICEMEN.
Go to #20 on the map.

6. 6 bones have to be removed.
Go to #18 on the map.

W	H	I	S	P	E	R
P	Y	T	H	I	A	N
D	E	R	A	N	G	E
A	N	G	R	I	L	Y
T	A	C	K	L	E	R

7. Miss Burnet's train was at 12:10 P.M.
For the trains to come at regular intervals, within 24 hours, they have to come every 4 hours and 45 minutes. Thus, we have the following times: 12:25 - 5:10 - 9:55 - 2:40 - 7:25 - 12:10. As to whether these times are A.M. or P.M., we refer to the policeman's account, which says that the event took place "during the day." It must therefore be 12:10 P.M.
POSEIDON: POISONED. *Go to #19 on the map.*

8. FALSE ALIBI. Mr. Scott Eccles' role was to give Garcia a false alibi, without realizing it, of course. Seventh column down reads MAGNETISED (the UK spelling of MAGNETIZED). *Go to #3 on the map.*

9. REVENGE is on Miss Burnet's mind. The word in the middle: TRAIN. *Go to #7 on the map.*

```
E A T E N
V R   △
E V A D E
N △   C
T △ N G E
R E V E N G E
```

```
B R I E F E M U R
P A N D A P A R T
E A S E L E G A L
A L I A S E N S E
S E R I E V E R Y
T I B I A F T E R
T I D A L A I T Y
C O A T I S S U E
B L U R B E E C H
C H I L I O D I N
```

10. Portrait 9.
Hair like 14, eyes like 4, nose like 2, mouth like 3, beard like 10. *Go to #22 on the map.*

11. The name of the owner and the name of the house both have a double letter. The double letter of the name comes alphabetically just before the double letter of the house. The one exception is Sir Clive Hammersmith of Old Fatham Hall, in which the double letter of the house precedes the double letter of the name. *Go to #21 on the map.*

12. JACKAL. *Go to #2 on the map.*

13. 1. No. All the people who left before breakfast at Wisteria Lodge were foreigners, but those who live elsewhere are not necessarily foreigners.
2. No. All foreigners are shady characters, but not all shady characters are foreigners.
3. No. All the people who live at Wisteria Lodge disappeared before breakfast, but people who do not live at Wisteria Lodge can also disappear before breakfast.
4. Yes. All the people living at Wisteria Lodge disappeared before breakfast, those who disappeared before breakfast are foreigners, and all foreigners are shady characters.
Go to #4 on the map.

14. 12 different routes. There are 6 different ways of spelling out V-O-O-D. From each D, there are 2 different ways of spelling D-O-O. *Go to #24 on the map.*

15. PARSLEY is the only plant. The other anagrams: HORNET, SNAKE, TORTOISE, PARROT, POODLE. *Go to #6 on the map.*

16.

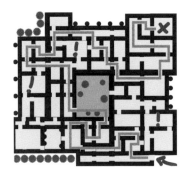

Go to #9 on the map.

17. BELGIUM. His route: FRANCE - HUNGARY - RUSSIA - SPAIN - UKRAINE - GERMANY - BELGIUM. The absent vowel from these country names: O. *Go to #14 on the map.*

18.

Fontheim	18045
Chalders	23604
Prescot	17113
Solweazy	20966
Parchet	18237
Total	97965

Go to #8 on the map.

19. Mocks/chains, will/free: Who mocks his chains will not be free.
Better/free, king/bird: Better a free bird than a king in captivity.
It/captivity, in/to: It is better to work and be free than to be fed in captivity.
Those/others, freedom/themselves: Those who deny freedom to others deserve it not for themselves.
They/others, drag/free: They are not free who drag their chains behind them.
Go to #5 on the map.

20. Policemen should be placed at 4, 5, and 11.
Go to #17 on the map.

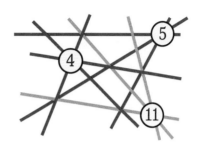

21. Faces E and J. *Go to #15 on the map.*

22. When Garcia called, it was in fact just after midnight, 12:05 A.M.
Garcia said it was 1 A.M. Scott Eccles' watch read 12:10 A.M. (50 minutes earlier).
But his watch was 15 minutes fast (according to the church clock), so the watch should have shown 11:55 P.M. Except that the church clock is 10 minutes slow, so Scott Eccles' watch should have shown 12:05 A.M. *Go to #13 on the map.*

23. 1. Mr. Lucas 2. Mr. Henderson 3. Miss Burnet 4. The girls.
Mr. Henderson is either in an orange room or a green room. If Mr. Henderson is in an orange room (1 or 3), then Miss Burnet is in a room with three windows (1 or 4), and if Miss Burnet's room has three windows, so does Mr. Lucas' room (1 or 4). Therefore, Mr. Henderson is in 3, Mr. Lucas in 1, and Miss Burnet in 4, which leaves the girls in 2. Since this room has a window looking south, then Lucas is in a green room, 4, and Miss Burnett is in 1. This means that Miss Burnet and the girls are next to each other, so Mr. Lucas should be in an orange room, which is NOT the case. Therefore, Mr. Henderson is NOT in an orange room. If Mr. Henderson is in a green room, the girls are in a green room also (2 and 4). The girls cannot be in 2 (window looking south), because that would mean with Mr. Lucas being in a green room, none are available. So, the girls must be in 4 and Mr. Henderson in 2. This means that Miss Burnet and Mr. Lucas are in the orange rooms (1 and 3), but Miss Burnet cannot be in 1, for it has three windows, which places Mr. Lucas in 4, which is not available. Therefore, Miss Burnet is in 3 and Mr. Lucas in 1. *Go to #12 on the map.*

24.

Boarish 5	Mortiferous 2
Corrupt 8	Noxious 6
Covetous 7	Rapacious 4
Ill-natured 1	Tyrannical 3

Answers to The Second Stain

1. 1. In favor. The anti abolishers are in favor of capital punishment. The opposition movement is against it. The foreign secretary cannot but reprove (he condemns) this movement; therefore, he is in favor of capital punishment.

2. Can go ahead. The project can be done (it is feasible) because it rests on sound ground. Some people doubt that this is so (they query it). But the foreign secretary disagrees with them (he has objections to these people). If he disagrees with those who doubt it, he does not doubt it, and therefore, he thinks this project can be carried out.

3. Would trust the medicine. Smith claims that the test, which was to establish that the medicine is safe, came up with negative results and that this result can be trusted (it is conclusive)—i.e., Smith thinks that this medicine is not safe. The foreign secretary thinks he is wrong, so he thinks the medicine is safe.

Go to #11 on the map.

2. Combination number: 15463.

In the first addition problem, one can see that the red circles cannot be 1, 2, or 3. They cannot be 4, in that there are not enough different combinations of numbers that add up to 4. They cannot be 5, in that the two identical numbers in the middle (green) can only add up to an even number. They can only be 6, so green is 3. Therefore, the yellow circle must be an even number, either 2 or 4, but the total result of that sum cannot be 22, so it must be 44, etc.

132+534=666 // 12+32=44 // 42+13=55. *Go to #19 on the map.*

3.

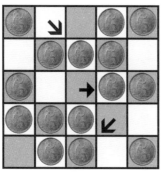

Go to #20 on the map.

4. One of many possibilities:

S	I	N	G	L	E
L	E	G	I	O	N
O	B	L	I	G	E
B	O	I	L	E	D
D	O	U	B	L	E

C	L	E	V	E	R
R	E	V	E	L	S
V	E	R	S	E	D
D	E	S	E	R	T
D	R	I	E	S	T
S	U	I	T	E	D
S	T	U	P	I	D

Go to #23 on the map.

5. Each number must be replaced by the corresponding number in Roman numerals: 1=I, 5=V, 10=X, 50=L, 100=C, 500=D, 1000=M. The upside-down 5=V turned upside-down, which represents an A. The upside-down 1000=M turned upside-down, which represents a W.
The text reads ALL CALM AMID MAD VILLA CLIMAX. LADI ILDA WILL CALL DAVID. One interprets "VILLA CLIMAX" as being the murder of Eduardo Lucas in his private house. LADI ILDA clearly stands for Lady Hilda. *Go to #7 on the map.*

6. Lucas' position is in carriage 22, that is 8 carriages after Dick's and 6 carriages before Tom's. Harry's position is in carriage 33: there are 32 carriages in front and 16 carriages behind. Dick's position is in carriage 13: there are 12 carriages in front and 36 carriages behind. Tom's position is in carriage 29: between carriages 13 and 33 are 19 carriages, so there are 15 carriages between Dick and Tom, and 3 carriages between Tom and Harry. *Go to #9 on the map.*

7. Keys 6 and 9. *Go to #15 on the map.*   **8.** Stamps 13, 31, and 32. *Go to #13 on the map.*

9. The clock and watch help Sherlock check that the valet is telling the truth, but they are not necessary in finding the answer. The valet set his watch on time at 10 A.M. It read 20 minutes past midnight when he came into the house. So according to the watch, 14 hours and 20 minutes had elapsed since 10 A.M. Because it gains 2 minutes every hour, the real time was 28, almost 29, minutes earlier. So, the valet arrived at the crime scene at 11:52 P.M. (The real time at which the clocks are shown is between 12:44 and 12:45.) *Go to #4 on the map.*

10. BLACKMAIL. *Go to #5 on the map.*

11. The missing pair: ♠ ⬠ Every pair of symbols appears first in one order and then in inverted order (square-circle/circle-square). Each of these pairs also appears with inverted colors (yellow-blue/blue-yellow). *Go to #17 on the map.*

12. All are correct but the first statement: Horace is the prime minister's father-in-law, but not Lady Hilda's uncle. He is the son of her grand-uncle.
Go to #16 on the map.

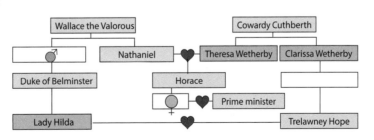

13. On one hand, Lucas or Oberstein is the oldest of the three, and on the other hand, Oberstein or La Rothière is the oldest. So, Oberstein must be the oldest. Then, according to the first statement, Oberstein is less wealthy than Lucas, and according to the third statement, he is wealthier than La Rothière. Thus, Lucas is the wealthiest, followed by Oberstein, and then La Rothière. With the the last statement, Lucas is older than La Rothière, so Oberstein is the oldest, followed by Lucas, and then La Rothière. Taking into account the second and fourth statements, the journalist is not La Rothière, who is the least wealthy of the three, and he is not Oberstein who is the oldest. The journalist is therefore Lucas. He is younger than the businessman, and Lucas is only younger than Oberstein. So, Oberstein is the businessman, and La Rothière is the art dealer. *Go to #3 on the map.*

14. LEONARD. The initials come in the order: EA - AL - AO - LE - ND - NO - OD. Only A and O appear three times, once together. The only initials with neither A nor O are LE and ND. *Go to #10 on the map.*

15. Safe number combination: 12618.
One has to find a horse bearing a number that is twice that of another horse and a third horse that has a number equal to the sum of the first two. *Go to #18 on the map.*

16. THE FAIR SEX IS YOUR DEPARTMENT WATSON. WHAT DID THE LADY REALLY WANT? *Go to #6 on the map.*

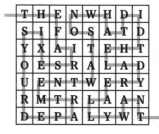

17. SERBIA. 1. SARAJEVO 2. BERLIN 3. WARSAW 4. LISBON 5. MADRID 6. TIRANA. *Go to #8 on the map.*

18. There is a total of 19 envelopes—12 envelopes before the letter and 6 after. Starting with the stamped letter, you move round 12 letters until you reach the first again. A group of 7 letters is left, and one has to be taken before removing the others. This is the precious letter. *Go to #24 on the map.*

19. 1. Thursday 2. Friday 3. Tuesday 4. Monday 5. Wednesday.
The Monday visitor is between two others and not in a striped dress, so she is 3 or 4. The Wednesday visitor is next to her and at one end, so she must be 5. So, Monday is 4 and Tuesday 3. The Thursday visitor is next to the striped dress, so she is 1, which leaves Friday for 2. *Go to #21 on the map.*

20. The little dagger. *Go to #12 on the map.*

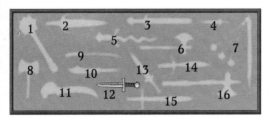

21.

T	O	W	E	R		A	M	P	L	E
A		O		E		D		A		A
P	A	R	T	S		M	E	R	I	T
E		D		T		I		K		E
R	A	S	P	S		T	R	A	I	N

Go to #14 on the map.

22. *Go to #2 on the map.*

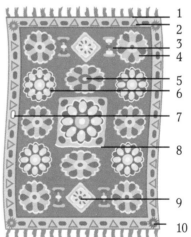

23.
1. Possible
2. Possible
3. Possible
4. No (All tenors are jealous, jealous people are liars.)
5. Possible
6. No (All spies are unfaithful.)
Go to #22 on the map.

24. THE LETTER WAS FOUND BECAUSE IT WAS NEVER LOST.

Answers to The Reigate Puzzle

1. Possible answers for choosing each card as the odd one out:

Two of clubs: This is the only card to have as face value a number that is a prime number. (Insofar as the queen has a face value, it is generally taken to be 12.) Less satisfactory, it is the only number under six (but such reasons can be stretched ad absurdum—only number between seven and nine, etc.).

Six of spades: This is the only card that is not symmetrical.

Eight of diamonds: This is the only card with a red suit, and is the only card with a suit that appears just once.

Ten of clubs: This is the only card whose value (or rank) is indicated with two figures. (Humph, the least satisfactory of answers.)

Queen of spades: This is the only court card.

You may have found other reasons. For them to be valid, they have to be generic and not specific (e.g., the only spades that is not a court card). *Go to #6 on the map.*

2.

Go to #8 on the map.

3. Malplaquet: 1709
Agincourt: 1415
Trafalgar: 1805
Shrewsbury: 1403
San Romano: 1432

In Sherlock's mnemonic phrases, the first two letters of the words give the corresponding number: NA for naught, ON for one, TW for two, TH for three, and so on.

Even without being an expert on dates, it is fair to assume that in Sherlock's time, most dates will start with 1, and the repeated first word beginning with ON should have put you on the right track. *Go to #16 on the map.*

4.

			A							
E		H		S	L	A	Y			F
X		O		S			C			E
E	L	I	M	I	N	A	T	E		R	L
C		I		S			K	I	L	L
U		C		S				M		
T		L	I	Q	U	I	D	A	T	E	G
I		D		N						A
O		E		C	A	R	N	A	G	E	S
N				T						H
	M	U	R	D	E	R	E	R		

S T R A N G U L A T I O N *Go to #2 on the map.*

5. There are 24 bricks missing. *Go to #9 on the map.*

6. RESILIENT. The words in the circles: ENERGY, STAMINA, HEALTH, STURDY, STRONG, FEISTY, ROBUST, FITNESS, HEARTY. *Go to #20 on the map.*

7. The family owns eight fields, four barns, the house, one pond, and the woods. This is the only combination that allows each one to be correct on two counts and false on one. One can proceed by elimination. If the first person is wrong about the house, then he is right about the seven fields and four barns, but then the third person is wrong on two counts. Impossible. If the first person is wrong about the four barns, then the second person is wrong also, but they do not agree on the number of fields, which means that one or the other is wrong on more than one point. Finally, one finds that the person at the top is wrong on the number of fields. *Go to #18 on the map.*

8. If one straightens out the switches in a line and indicates a light that is on with an O and a light that is off with an F, one starts with F **O** F F F O F. If one switches the two underlined switches, this gives F **F O** F F O F, followed by F F F **O F** O F, then F F F F F **O O** F, and finally F F F F F F F. *Go to #11 on the map.*

9. SWOON, FAINT, DIZZY, GIDDY, SHAKY. *Go to #14 on the map.*

10. Each letter corresponds to the town beginning with that letter: A-B-D-G, A-B-H-I, A-B-H-K, A-C-D-I, A-C-D-G, A-C-D-K, A-F-K-I, B-C-D-H, D-G-I-H, D-G-K-H, D-H-J-L, I-J-L-K, etc. *Go to #3 on the map.*

11. Four different structures altogether: 4, 8, and 10 are unique, and all the others are identical. *Go to #17 on the map.*

12. Holmes was describing a telephone (of that time). The text: "This apparatus has only recently been patented in the United States of America, but I trust it will enter most of our homes before long. It comes in three parts. One which stands on the desk with a little winding handle on the side and two parts which you can hold in either hand. In one of these you can talk, while you take the other to your ear. This contraption allows you to converse with people who can be quite some distance away." *Go to #15 on the map.*

Answers to The Reigate Puzzle

13.

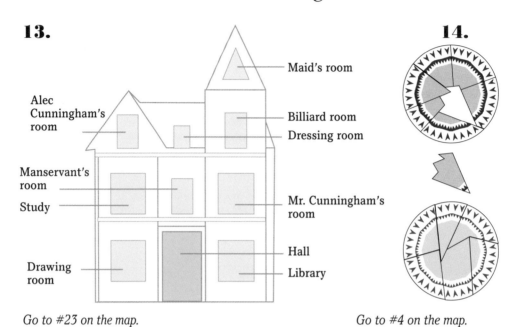

Maid's room

Alec Cunningham's room

Billiard room

Dressing room

Manservant's room

Study

Mr. Cunningham's room

Drawing room

Hall

Library

Go to #23 on the map.

14.

Go to #4 on the map.

15. Odd word out: FAMILY. The other words: APPOINTMENT, ASSEMBLY, ASSOCIATION, AUDIENCE, CAUCUS, CONCLAVE, CONFERENCE, CONGREGATION, CONGRESS, CONSULTATION, CONVENTION, COUNCIL, ENCOUNTER, GATHERING, INTERVIEW, MEETING, REUNION, SEMINAR, SYMPOSIUM. *Go to #7 on the map.*

16. The coachman's score is 85 (blue=10, red=18, yellow=25), which incidentally means that Alec Cunningham did NOT have the top score, as he suggests.

The third target on the left side must have an even score (two arrows in two sections); therefore, the score is either 56 or 78. If it were 78, however, the sum of the blue and red sections would be 39, and this (without going into details) is impossible when applied to the other two targets on the left side. Therefore, the third target on the left scores 56, making the sum of the blue and red sections 28. If the second target on the left scores 63, we again come to an impossibility (63 - 28=35, making the value of the yellow section 17.5, an unlikely value and incompatible with the next target). The second target on the left must then be worth 78 and the yellow bull's-eye 50 (78 - 28=50), making the value for each yellow arrow 25. The score of the first target on the left must then be 63 (blue+red=28 and yellow=25), which means the last blue arrow=10. *Go to #5 on the map.*

17.

T	H	R	O	W	N	E	R	S
R	A	M	P	A	R	T	I	C	L	E
J	A	V	E	L	I	N	O	C	U	T
M	A	J	E	S	T	Y	L	I	S	H
A	C	R	Y	L	I	C	E	N	C	E
A	N	C	I	E	N	T	I	T	L	E
C	A	B	B	A	G	E	N	D	A	S

Go to #22 on the map.

18. For those of you who are familiar with "The Reigate Puzzle" story, the solution will not have been too difficult. The culprits in this instance have used exactly the same trick to mislead the handwriting experts. There were two people who wrote the note, with each one writing every other word. On examining the handwriting carefully, you will find that the first word, along with every other following word, was written by Margaret Freize, and that the words in between were written by Adrian Buckley. Compare, in particular, the letters that appear in both their names: a, e, i, r. *Go to #21 on the map.*

19. SPASM. The other words: HOSED, CASTS, MASTS, PAPER, WIPED, RIPEN, BEACH, STACK, SHARE, LASER, GISTS, DUSTS, DIMES, CAMPS, LIMIT. *Go to #24 on the map.*

20.

Go to #12 on the map.

21. This is what the text should look like without typos: Dear Sir, Could we arrange to meet somewhere close to the station next week? I suggest Saturday at twelve o'clock. Would that suit you? Sincerely yours. Underline every mistyped letter for the hidden message: Enter by back door. Key in red jar. Map clue: For your next destination on the map, go to House Plans. *Go to #13 on the map.*

22.

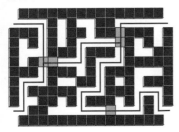

Go to #19 on the map.

23. The first name of the servant begins with the last three letters of his function, and the family name begins with the first two of the function. PERdita HOrn is the HOusekeePER, ANThony MAson is the MAnservANT, AIDa MAson is the MAID, and MANuel FOx is the FOotMAN. Therefore, TERry POsher must be the POrTER. *Go to #10 on the map.*

24.

Answers to The Greek Interpreter

1.

The letters that are not included in any word spell BROTHER. *Go to #18 on the map.*

2. Below are the counters in the right slots, showing the letters on the back.
Following Holmes' intuition: TRIFLE.
S+1=T, P+2=R, F+3=I, B+4=F, G+5=L, Y+6=E.
Go to #14 on the map.

3. The price of the missing set is £38:
carving fork = £8; spoon = £6; knife = £5; fork = £4; teaspoon = £3.

- £28 set + £20 set: 4 carving forks + 4 normal forks = £48, which means a carving fork + fork = £12.
- £24 set without the carving fork + fork (£24 - £12) leaves 2 spoons = £12, which means a spoon = £6.
- £20 set without the carving fork + fork (£20 - £12) leaves 2 forks = £8, which means a fork = £4.
- £28 set without the carving fork and fork (£28 - £12) leaves 2 carving forks = £16, which means a carving fork = £8.
- £18 set without a carving fork (£18 - £8) leaves 2 knives = £10, which means a knife = £5.
- £22 set: carving fork + spoon + knife = £19, which means 1 teaspoon = £3. *Go to #16 on the map.*

4. The four interpreters: 3, 5, 2, 13. Greek - 3 (Greek, French) - 5 (French, Croatian) - 2 (Croatian, Italian) - 13 (Italian, English) - English. *Go to #10 on the map.*

5. PLEASE SEND ALL INFORMATION CONCERNING THE GREEK CITIZEN KRATIDES TO 221B BAKER ST. *Go to #23 on the map.*

6. 25,004 yards, or 14 miles and 364 yards.
The wheel went around 56 times per minute, so 56 x 4.7 (the wheel's circumference) = 263.2 yards per minute. The journey lasted 95 minutes, so it traveled 95 x 263.2.
Go to #13 on the map.

7. Jenkins has 12 monocycles, 6 bicycles, and 4 tricycles.
If M stands for monocycle, B for bicycle, and T for tricycle, then we know that
M+B=24 wheels, M+T=24 wheels, and B+T=24 wheels.
Therefore, M=B=T=12 wheels. *Go to #11 on the map.*

8. Clock 4. 9 has no pendulum, 6 has a pendulum but it isn't round, 2 has visible weights, 3 doesn't have the same time, 8 has little feet, 10 has a visible name, 1 has Roman numerals, 5 is the tallest, and 7 is the shortest. *Go to #5 on the map.*

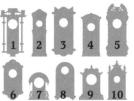

9. 1. bicycle 2. light carriage 3. handcart 4. wheelbarrow 5. heavy carriage. Inspector Gregson's statement is incompatible with Barry's (the heavy carriage couldn't be last and have the light carriage come after). Inspector Gregson's statement is also incompatible with Sherlock Holmes' statement (Gregson says two vehicles preceded the heavy carriage, which leaves two to follow; Holmes says three followed). Therefore, the mistaken statement has been made by Inspector Gregson.
Go to #3 on the map.

10. The first frieze can be divided into five identical sections. The second can be divided into five sections, each one having three spaces between the decorations. The third frieze can be divided into five sections, each one containing a red spot. The fourth frieze can be divided into five sections, each one containing shapes having a total of ten sides.
Go to #6 on the map.

11. The single footprint belongs to ART (bottom row, second from the left). His name must therefore be ARTHUR. The other pairs: ALBERT, ALFRED, ANDREW, ARNOLD, ERNEST, GEORGE, HAROLD, HUBERT, JOSEPH, MARTIN, THOMAS.
Go to #4 on the map.

12. If the house numbers are in a regular numerical progression, as is the case on many London roads, there are four possible solutions: six on the dotted line for 1+2+3+4+5+6=21, and the house is 7; three on the dotted line for 6+7+8=21, and the house is 9; two on the dotted line for 10+11=21, and the house is 12; and one on the dotted line for 21, and the house is 22 (but the plural "numbers" is wrong).
If the house numbers are odd on one side and even on the other, write three on the dotted line for 5+7+9=21, and the house is 10. *Go to #17 on the map.*

13. Portrait 5. *Go to #22 on the map.*

14. Holmes either brought a jackknife or he didn't. If he did bring a jackknife, Barry brought a revolver. Therefore, Watson didn't bring a dagger (for that would mean that Barry came with a cudgel). So, then Watson must have come with a cudgel and the inspector with the dagger. But we arrive at a contradiction, for if the inspector came with a dagger, then Watson should have come with a jackknife, but comes with a cudgel instead. So, Holmes didn't bring a jackknife, and that means that Watson came with a dagger. If Watson came with a dagger and Barry a cudgel, this leaves the inspector with the jackknife and Holmes with the revolver. *Go to #20 on the map.*

15. Mycroft would rather be considered wrong than take the trouble to prove himself right.
Go to #7 on the map.

16. English authors are bound in green, Roman authors in red, and Greek authors in yellow. But there's a volume of Shelley, an English poet, bound in yellow—a disgrace that Holmes could spot a mile away. *Go to #24 on the map.*

17. DAHLIA. Other flowers: LUPIN, IRIS, DAISY, HEATHER, ASTER, ANEMONE.
Go to #2 on the map.

18. From left to right: Bartholomew, Thaddeus, Mycroft, Obediah, Reuben, Enoch. Note that "to Reuben's right" means on Reuben's right side, which means for one looking at them, to the left of Reuben. On the contrary, farther to the right means for one looking at them, to the right side. *Go to #21 on the map.*

19. HAMSTER - **CLA**RIFY - DE**CLA**RE - **HAM**LETS - **HAM**MERS - C**HAM**BER - **CLA**WING - **CLA**NGER - S**HAM**BLE - E**CLA**IRS. *Go to #8 on the map.*

20.

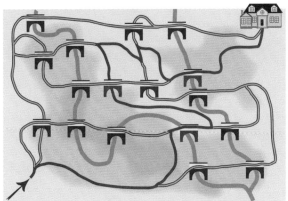

Go to #9 on the map.

21. Nine of clubs. *Go to #15 on the map.*

22. Hidden message: My name is Paul Kratides.
The missing letters: no a**M**ount of miser**Y** ca**N** m**A**ke **M**e agre**E** to the**I**r devili**S**h **P**lans. wh**A**tever they make me s**U**ffer, I shal**L** resist, **K**nowing pe**R**fectly well th**A**t **T**hey are ruthless indiv**I**duals an**D** that th**E**y may **S**lay me. Map clue: **N**obody **I**s **N**egotiating, not **E**ven **T**he **E**xtremely **E**nvious **N**oblemen. *Go to #19 on the map.*

23. Sophy, a Greek girl, comes on a visit to England, // and this man, Harold, persuades her to flee // with him. Then her brother comes over from // Greece and imprudently puts himself into the // power of the young man and his associate. // They use violence towards him in order to // make him sign some papers to make over // the girl's fortune. This he refuses to do. In // order to negotiate with him they have to //get an interpreter and choose Mr. Melas. Map clue: Two multiplied by six is the number of your next destination. *Go to #12 on the map.*

24. SOPHY HAS TAKEN HER REVENGE. The first letter, S, is the first S when moving counterclockwise from the top, and then the message can also be read counterclockwise.

Answers to The Bruce-Partington Plans

1. 1. E, 9:55 2. C, 10:09 3. A, 10:34 4. F, 10:57 5. B, 11:10 6. D, 11:23. *Go to #14 on the map.*

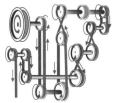

2. The belt moves downward. *Go to #7 on the map.*

3. The different cube is the one at the bottom left. If you look at the top-right and top-left cubes, each of their blue fleur-de-lis is pointing in the direction of a green symbol (that also contains a diminutive version of the fleur-de-lis). The bottom-left cube's blue fleur-de-lis isn't pointing at this green symbol but is parallel to it. *Go to #22 on the map.*

4. *Go to #19 on the map.*

5. 44, 30, and 21. *Go to #2 on the map.*

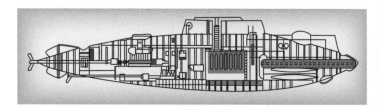

6. BRIGHT/DARK, CLEVER/STUPID, UNFAITHFUL/LOYAL, CAUTIOUS/CARELESS, DECEITFUL/SINCERE, TENACIOUS/IRRESOLUTE. MESPIGSENEONGERS: MESSENGER PIGEONS. *Go to #9 on the map.*

7. Sequence: A-F-H-B-I-D-G-C-E. *Go to #20 on the map.*

8. Odd word out: CLASSIFIED. The other words: CASTAWAY, DESERTED, DISCARDED, DITCHED, DROPPED, ESTRANGED, FORGOTTEN, FORSAKEN, JILTED, NEGLECTED, OSTRACIZED, REJECTED, REPUDIATED, STRANDED. *Go to #5 on the map.*

9. The busiest intersection is in the small, green country at the lower right (Serbia). *Go to #17 on the map.*

10. It is fortunate for this community that I am not a criminal (Sherlock Holmes in "The Bruce-Partington Plans"). It is a mercy that you are on the side of the force and not against it (Inspector Gregson in "The Greek Interpreter"). *Go to #21 on the map.*

11. Use the keys of Mr. Strickland, Mr. Freemont, Mr. Thrust, Mr. Clarence, and Mrs. Awnsight. *Go to #15 on the map.*

12. To find the hidden message, you must combine all the double letters in the order in which they appear. The first message: Come at four (acceptance - too - imminent - foresee - Isaacs - omitted - unaffordable - goods - vacuum - override).
The second message: Meet in flat (Jimmy - Green - week's - attractive - skiing - planning - offer - full - bazaar - little). *Go to #24 on the map.*

13. Lamp, £7; mallet, £3; chisel, £5; revolver, £18. *Go to #23 on the map.*

14. Both grids: LASSUS.
Left grid: ARSANTIQUA, BAROQUE, BASS, CANON, CHOIR, EARTHLY, GREGORIAN, JOSQUIN, LASSUS, MACHAUT, MADRIGAL, MODES, MOTET, PALESTRINA, PIPES, QUEEN, RECORDER, RONDEAU, SACRED, VOCAL.
Right grid: ARSNOVA, CANTICLES, DULCIMER, INSTRUMENTAL, LASSUS, LUTE, OCTAVE, ORGANUM, PIPES, PLAINCHANT, POLYPHONIC, SECULAR, SONG, TROUBADORS, TROUVERE, VICTORIA. *Go to #10 on the map.*

```
P I P E S B X X     A R S N O V A I
X M A C H A U T     S X R C V P X N
L Y L H T R A E     O T U A I O T S
U A E D N O R T     N R O N C L N T
G R S X E Q E O     G O D T T Y A R
R S T S E U D M     X U A I O P H U
E A R X U E R X     R V B C R H C M
G N I U Q S O J     E E U L I O N E
O T N O N A C S     M R O E A N I N
R I A M O D E S     I E R S X I A T
I Q C H O I R A     C E T U L C L A
A U L A C O V B     L A S S U S P L
N A D E R C A S     U M U N A G R O
M A D R I G A L     D S E C U L A R
```

15. From left to right: Sergio Malavista, Adolph Meyer, Hugo Oberstein, Piotr Volovitch, Louis La Rothière. *Go to #8 on the map.*

16. DON'T OPEN. POISONED. *Go to #3 on the map.*

17. From left to right, the weights from lightest to heaviest. By "combining" sets of scales and then eliminating the same color bottles that are on either side, one can establish successively the relative weights of all the bottles.
Go to #12 on the map.

```
P O D O
O I S P
E O N N
E T N D
```

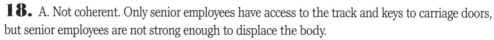

18. A. Not coherent. Only senior employees have access to the track and keys to carriage doors, but senior employees are not strong enough to displace the body.

B. Not coherent. The absence of blood means that either the body has been moved or the crime took place earlier. But the body cannot have been moved for the same reason as above: only senior employees have access, and they are not strong enough to move the body. The absence of blood could mean that the crime took place before the body was thrown out of the carriage, but no evidence of violence was found in any carriage.

C. Not coherent. There's no evidence of violence in any carriage.

D. Not coherent, for the reasons given above.

E. Coherent. Clearly another explanation must be found (and guess who will find it?). *Go to #13 on the map.*

19. Left: 1. F. W. Karsley 2. P. J. Harmond 3. S. A. Maximus 4. O. D. Johnsteen
Center: 1. R. H. Raphaels 2. P. J. Harmond 3. B. B. Debs 4. S. A. Maximus
Right: 1. F. W. Karsley 2. R. H. Raphaels 3. C. U. Creight 4. P. J. Harmond
Go to #11 on the map.

20. When all other contingencies fail, whatever remains, however improbable, must be the truth. *Go to #18 on the map.*

21. At Westminster take the Westbound train at 7:53. Get off at Victoria at 8:08. Take the Eastbound train at 8:27. Get off at Cannon Street at 9:25 and take the Westbound train at 9:27. Get off at Mansion House at 9:31. Get on an Eastbound train again at 9:34. Arrive at Algate at 9:57. *Go to #4 on the map.*

22. The writing on the fence was: POLICE WATCH OUT! EVEN IF YOU TRY TO COVER UP, SHERLOCK HOLMES WILL REVEAL ALL THE REAL FACTS.
(1-15-2-3-6-7-4-9-10-16-13-17-11-8-14-12-5-18). *Go to #6 on the map.*

23. The three words: VISITING, BURGLARY, UNLAWFUL. *Go to #16 on the map.*

24. Starting with the pin with the large oval stone at the top of the circle and moving clockwise, Sherlock Holmes' tiepin is the seventh one down, with a round stone encircled in gold on a gold pin (between a square and an oblong stone).

Answers to The Sherlock Challenge

The Grids

1

C	H	A	N	C	E
H	E	A	L	T	H
E	A	S	I	L	Y
S	T	R	I	N	G
T	E	A	P	O	T
P	R	A	I	S	E

2

B	O	U	N	C	E
E	L	D	E	R	S
R	A	T	T	L	E
M	O	R	S	E	L
S	A	N	I	T	Y
E	A	G	L	E	S

3

S	A	I	L	O	R
L	I	K	E	L	Y
A	D	M	I	R	E
S	T	A	P	L	E
F	A	M	I	L	Y
A	C	T	I	V	E

4

M	E	D	I	U	M
D	I	A	L	O	G
B	I	T	T	E	R
C	O	H	O	R	T
W	E	A	L	T	H
R	I	D	D	L	E

5

P	E	N	C	I	L
E	N	E	R	G	Y
V	I	K	I	N	G
I	R	O	N	I	C
L	E	N	G	T	H
P	A	C	K	E	T

6

O	C	C	U	P	Y
N	I	N	E	T	Y
T	O	F	F	E	E
T	A	I	L	O	R
C	H	A	I	R	S
S	U	B	T	L	E

Hidden Words

Chapter 1

H	E	A	T	E	R
1	2	3	4	5	6

Chapter 2

L	I	S	T	E	N
7	8	9	10	11	12

Chapter 3

S	I	M	P	L	E
13	14	15	16	17	18

Chapter 4

M	O	T	H	E	R
19	20	21	22	23	24

Chapter 5

I	G	N	I	T	E
25	26	27	28	29	30

Chapter 6

S	H	I	F	T	Y
31	32	33	34	35	36

The Sherlock Quote

"It has long been an axiom of mine that . . . "

T	H	E
29	22	11

L	I	T	T	L	E
7	14	4	35	17	23

T	H	I	N	G	S
21	32	8	12	26	13

A	R	E
3	24	30

I	N	F	I	N	I	T	E	L	Y
25	12	34	28	27	33	10	5	17	36

T	H	E
4	22	30

M	O	S	T
19	20	31	10

I	M	P	O	R	T	A	N	T
25	19	16	20	24	35	3	12	4

Answers to The Map Challenge

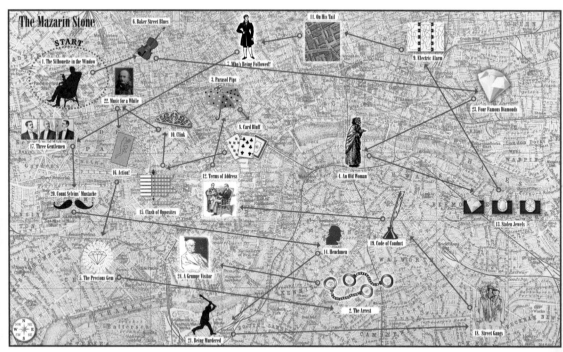

The Mazarin Stone

1. The Silhouette in the Window
2. The Arrest
3. Parasol Pips
4. An Old Woman
5. The Precious Gem
6. Baker Street Blues
7. Who's Being Followed?
8. Card Bluff
9. Electric Alarm
10. Clink
11. On His Tail
12. Terms of Address
13. Stolen Jewels
14. Henchmen
15. Clash of Opposites
16. Action!
17. Three Gentlemen
18. Street Gangs
19. Code of Conduct
20. Count Sylvius' Mustache
21. Being Murdered
22. Music for a While
23. Four Famous Diamonds
24. A Grumpy Visitor

START

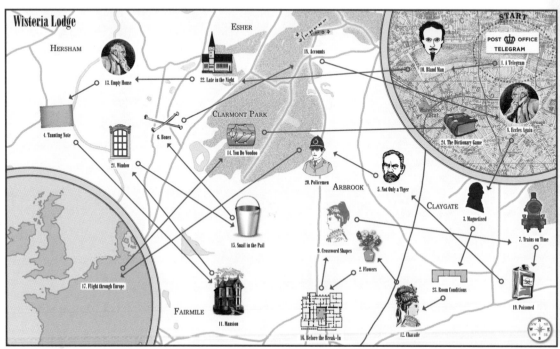

Wisteria Lodge

1. A Telegram
2. Flowers
3. Magnetised
4. Taunting Note
5. Not Only a Tiger
6. Bones
7. Trains on Time
8. Eccles Again
9. Crossword Shapes
10. Bland Man
11. Mansion
12. Charade
13. Empty House
14. You Do Voodoo
15. Snail in the Pail
16. Before the Break-In
17. Flight through Europe
18. Accounts
19. Poisoned
20. Policemen
21. Window
22. Late in the Night
23. Room Conditions
24. The Dictionary Game

HERSHAM
ESHER
CLARMONT PARK
ARBROOK
CLAYGATE
FAIRMILE

START

POST OFFICE
TELEGRAM

The Second Stain

- START
- 12. Family Tree
- 20. Shadow of a Crime
- 3. Penny Patience
- 2. Number Combination
- 1. Gobbledygook
- 22. Carpet Symmetry
- 9. The Valet's Alibi
- 13. Master Spies
- 7. Duplicate Key
- 11. Stolen Letter
- 14. Coded Initials
- 19. Lady Visitor
- 15. Hunting
- 4. Changing Personality
- 23. Crazy Logic
- 21. Two Explanations
- 5. Roman Message
- 6. Spies on a Train
- 8. Postage
- 16. Lady Hilda
- 24. To Conclude
- 10. Culprit or Victim?
- 18. Precious Letter
- 17. Potentate

The Reigate Puzzle

- WESTHUMBLE
- 2. Family Claims
- 5. Gap in the Wall
- 9. Diversion
- 14. Cracked Crockery
- 4. Killers
- 11. Wooden Blocks
- MERSTHAM
- 10. House to House
- 15. Scrap of Paper
- 8. Light Lock
- 2. Bullets
- BUCKLAND
- 23. Domestic Staff
- REIGATE
- 3. Lintel
- REDHILL
- 13. House Plans
- 12. Murder
- 18. Handwriting
- 21. Typo
- 20. Robbery!
- START
- 16. Archery
- 6. Word Wheels
- 1. Solitaire
- 17. Sandwich
- LEIGH
- 22. Maze
- 19. Watson's Word
- SALFORDS
- 24. Chess Challenge

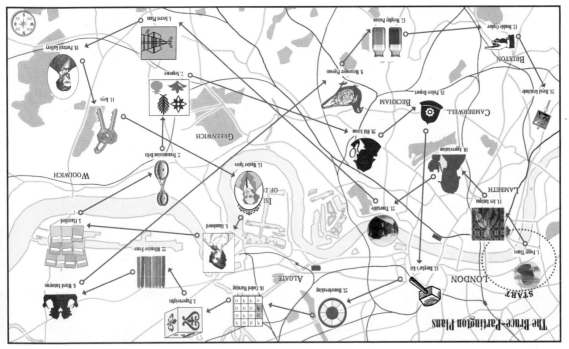

The Bruce-Partington Plans

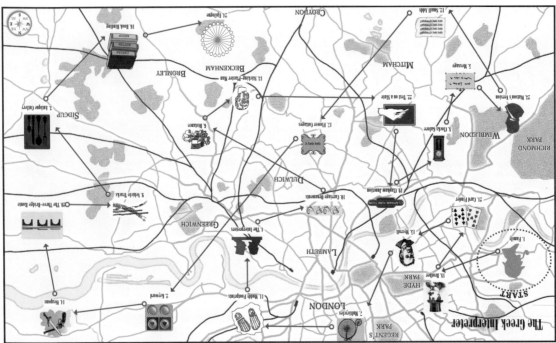

The Greek Interpreter